Keep Taxes Away from Your Wealth

5 Strategies To Reducing Taxes You Owe Now and Into the Future

Keep Taxes Away from Your Wealth

**5 Strategies To Reducing Taxes
You Owe Now and Into the Future**

Henry Wong, Jayson Lowe, and Richard Canfield

Library of Congress Cataloging-in-Publication Data has been applied for

ISBN: 978-1-7781450-2-5

This book is dedicated to R. Nelson Nash

Keep Taxes Away from Your Wealth

Here's What's Inside:

ACCESS YOUR FREE GIFT!

READ THIS FIRST

As a thank you for subscribing to our book series, we're giving you a gift of access to our team and our supplemental resources so that you can start the process of Becoming Your Own Banker®, The Infinite Banking Concept®.

Your gift comes with the following:

- Connecting with an experienced authorized Infinite Banking practitioner on our team for a conversation to answer your questions and uncover how this process is best suited for you.
- A free trial account on our Client Success Portal gives you instant access to all our resources and coaching, on-demand, on any device, at your time of need.

TEXT THE WORD "SCHEDULE" TO: (844) 936 2656

wealthwithoutbaystreet.com/bonus

Meet the Authors

*"We believe that financial control should be in your hands,
not the banks, not the government, not the stock market."*
– Jayson Lowe, Richard Canfield

Henry Wong

I, like my co-authors, am inspired by the incredible R. Nelson Nash and his books, *Becoming Your Own Banker®* and *Building Your Warehouse of Wealth*. Before I was exposed to Nelson Nash, I followed all the mainstream conventional advice: investing in financial markets, real estate and building my own businesses. On the surface, everything looked great, as though I had it under control. I did not have it under control. My life was consumed by financial stresses, primarily making and keeping money.

Hence, I worked a tremendous number of hours to get ahead. I functioned under the theory that I would get ahead in life by increasing my income, expanding my income sources, and chasing the next significant investment. Initially, I assumed this was normal, given my youth and that it would all get better down the line. Until it didn't. And in 2016, I reached my breaking point. My theory wasn't working and no longer made sense to me.

Born in Canada to immigrant parents, I learned from the start the need to work hard and save wherever possible. My parents earned three dollars an hour, and as they struggled and sacrificed to provide me with a better life, tensions often rose in our home. With a front-row seat to how financial strife can negatively impact a family, I felt motivated as a young adult to figure out how to control my money, hence, my decision to become a Chartered Professional Accountant (CPA).

I began my CPA career with one of the big four accounting firms, advising large public, private, and owner-managed businesses in audit, tax, and advisory areas. But when the recession of 2008, and 2009 hit, I hit a defining moment. With businesses collapsing and lives altered forever, this marked a truly trying time for many. So shortly after, I began specializing in real estate businesses, mainly apartment complexes, real estate developments, hotels, and tax planning. This is when I saw the flip side of that financial downturn and witnessed flourishing industries as we emerged from the recession.

Eventually, I left my career at a big four accounting firm and accepted a position at Canada's largest telecom company as a controller managing money flow for a business with 400 million dollars of revenue. Yet, climbing the corporate ladder didn't fit into my overall vision for my future, so I ventured out on my own and became an entrepreneur creating and selling an ecommerce business.

After starting my own consulting, accounting, and advisory business, working with private companies and high net-worth families, I noticed each had one tool in their financial bag, one that I had never learned about in university or during my initial years in accounting. I noted this financial vehicle, but never understood how it connected to building wealth.

After my initial read of *Becoming Your Own Banker*®, admittingly, it took me a few years to employ Nelson's concepts. But once I did, my frustration with losing so much of my hard-earned cash dissipated, placing me in the driver's seat to manage the growth and protection of my wealth. I regret that I could never personally thank Nelson for changing my financial life.

My hard work and affinity to absorb as much knowledge through my professional pursuits and reading assisted my wealth accumulation over those years. But in 2015, my life took a dramatic turn—which I will discuss later—and I lost most of what I had accumulated. Still frustrated, but determined, I went on a three-year journey to learn how to trade in the financial markets and rebuild my cash warehouse.

Once again, financially healthy, I started to see how the Canadian government was siphoning my money away from me. There was nothing I could do about it. The more I made, the more they took—a matrix of systems designed by the government. To make matters worse, the government's often questionable spending and mismanagement created an inflationary economy for the hard-working, taxpaying citizens who deserved better.

It's precisely that angst that incentivized me to employ Nelson Nash's concepts to create and manage my wealth, protecting it from flowing out of my pocket into the hands of the Canadian government. So, inevitably, I met Jayson and Richard and joined their team by making those changes in my approach.

Together, we have worked on providing our clients with the incredible tool we will discuss in the upcoming chapters to not only create a place of wealth to legally store their capital to fund their lives but also to keep their wealth protected from the hands that want to take it away at every possible turn, the Canadian government.

The Power of Family Banking is Yours,

Henry Wong

Jayson Lowe and Richard Canfield

We are Jayson Lowe and Richard Canfield, co-authors of this book series. As children, we were impacted by financial difficulties within our families, experiencing money struggles firsthand. Having now achieved cash confidence and financial control as adults, we decided to write this book series to serve as an inspiration and a guide for others to create their own peaceful, stress-free way of life financially.

It was January 2010, a cold, snowy night in Edmonton, Alberta, when we began educating individuals on our financial process inside a boardroom no bigger than a closet. And from that tiny boardroom, our program evolved into evening and weekend events, packed each time with attendees from all across Canada.

You can register for our next training sessions here:
http://wwbstraining.com

Our educational series, live events, and webinars emanated from the principles we learned directly from the late R. Nelson Nash, author of the # 1 best-selling book *Becoming Your Own Banker*®. To date, Nelson's book has sold more than 500,000 copies and is self-published! Why? Because it works.

KEEP TAXES AWAY FROM YOUR WEALTH

Get your copy of Nelson's book here:
http://wealthwithoutbaystreet.com/books

In 2020, we launched our podcast, "Wealth Without Bay Street," to help our listeners understand how to control and build wealth without putting all of their capital at risk. Financial entertainers and the media encourage taking unnecessary risks in the market; it simply doesn't have to be that way.

And now, you're holding in your hands one book from a series that will open your mind to a whole new financial world.

And if you've read our introductory book, the *Canadian's Guide to Wealth Building Without Risk*, thank you. Plus, that means you know our backstory, so there is no need to repeat it. But, if you haven't read it, we highly recommend you do, as it will give you insights into who we are and how we approach building a peaceful, stress-free way of life financially.

Our focus is on helping people just like you to achieve that in your own life. We know that money will not buy happiness, but we also know that being broke won't buy you anything. Having more money and knowing how to keep that money in your family banking system can enable you to create the financial lifestyle that you want, versus reacting to the one that you already have. And by getting the bankers out of your life (or the snakes and dragons, as Nelson Nash often said), along with doing what drives you, you can live a more purposeful life. These elements are all key to a happier existence.

Most of all, we know that you will be inspired to act and follow our easy-to-implement and straightforward process. Therefore, continue reading with the understanding that knowledge can be inspiring, but it doesn't change a darn thing unless you act upon it with determination and perseverance. You've heard the saying, "How do you eat an elephant? One bite at a time." Consider the steps we outline in this book as taking small, easy-to-digest bites of your financial elephant. Don't stop until you reach your goals. We promise to be here as your guides along the way.

To Your Best Life,

Jayson and Richard

Chapter One

What You Don't Know Can Hurt You

"If you are the least bit effective in accumulating wealth, you are going to find yourself engulfed in taxation." – Jayson Lowe

---

Have you ever heard of Willie Sutton? He was an infamous bank robber in the early 1900's. A successful thief who stole an estimated two million dollars during his lifetime. Willie was finally arrested and charged in 1931 for his crimes. Although he escaped prison several times, he spent over half his life behind bars. Now, the interesting part was when a reporter, Mitch Ohnstad, asked Willie, "Why do you rob banks?" Willie replied, "Because that's where they keep all the money."

Ok, so yes, Willie wasn't brilliant; he just stated the obvious. However, if you read Jayson's quote at the top of this chapter, think about the simple message within Willie's words: If you have any money accumulating, you can bet someone else, namely the government and banks, are watching and together figuring out ways to get it. Malicious or not, the systems are designed to ensure you are not the sole beneficiary of your efforts.

Now, you have worked hard to build that capital and sacrificed to save for the future; why hand it over to someone else? And yes, I'm sure you are aware of a few ways to shelter your money from taxes, but not all methods—financial vehicles—are created equal.

For example, we had a client, Chris, who was self-employed, and to avoid so much of his income being taxed away from him, he put his money in a Registered Retirement Savings Plan (RRSP), or what we call the money prison because of its lack of accessibility and taxation penalties at withdrawal. Although Chris had the correct mindset to try and shelter his income from taxation, he chose the wrong vehicle. Yes, an RRSP will accumulate and protect him from taxes. However, if Chris was to pass away early, the Canadian government would take roughly 50%, or if he needed to withdraw his funds early, he would pay 30% with each withdrawal (withholding tax of 30% if withdrawing $15,000 or more). Then after the withdrawal, he would be subject to further tax as the entire amount is added to his annual income for the year. So, what did Chris do when he realized this risk? First, he came to see us, and later in this book, we will tell you how we turned his situation around to protect his money and give him total control over his wealth, not only for him but for all future generations.

Please understand we are not describing or advocating tax avoidance. That would be unlawful, and we would never support that. Taxes are necessary in order for a government to function. Onerous taxation is the disturbing element we're addressing here. And not all your tax dollars are spent to benefit you or the community where you live and work. When the money spent is not yours, you care less about it—it's human nature. Which is no different when the money is centralized into a system owned and controlled by a government. In fact, it creates a ripe environment for misuse. This means you hand over your money to the government with every transaction and pay cheque and have no say in where it goes.

But, what if we told you there are legal ways to minimize the taxable events in your life, increase and keep more of your wealth, all while being in a position of total financial control? How would that make you feel? Amazing? So, let's get started!

What's the Problem?

For a moment, oblige us and play along with the following scenario. Imagine you are a small start-up business owner. And as a business owner, your first year's (2014-2015) numbers look like this:

- Revenue $282.30
- Expenses $280.40
- Profit $1.90

Not very exciting, but profit is profit! Well, let's suppose you elect to bring on new management, and over the next five years, your numbers look as follows:

	2016-2017	2017-2018	2018-2019	2019-2020	2020-2021
Revenue	$293.50	$313.60	$332.20	$334.10	$316.40
Expenses	$312.50	$332.60	$337.80	$362.90	$628.90
Profit/Loss	$(19.00)	$(19.00)	$ (14.00)	$(39.40)	$(327.70)
Debt Accumulation	$1.12	$1.16	$1.19	$1.25	$1.65

Now, what would you think of this new management team? We suspect you'd be pretty upset. Well, what if we told you these numbers in our scenario are real and that they represent billions? Then what if we told you that this is a business you fund currently? And that the management team spends your hard-earned cash without your approval. Yes, these numbers represent the audited financial numbers of the Canadian government! The simple chart above represents what happened when the Trudeau administration took over from the previous government. Regardless of political leanings, let's agree this is very disturbing.

As depicted, within seven years, we started from a profit (surplus in government lingo) of $1.9 billion in 2014-2015 to a loss (deficit) in 2021 of $327.7 billion. As a result, total debt ballooned from $1 trillion to over 1.6 *trillion* dollars! Under the Harper government, even with the $1.9 billion surplus, it would take the current government 538 years to pay the debt back. Yet, since the Trudeau government took over, there doesn't seem to be any plans to pay this back. And guess who will pay for it? You and future generations including your family. Let's think about that for a second. If one generation is approximately 25 to 30 years, it will take 18 generations to pay off one trillion of federal debt.

Got your attention? Good.

So, let's do some math here; let's suppose the following:

- In Canada, at the time of writing this book, there are 38.7 million residents.
- Assume 30 million are working adults.
- The average Canadian salary is approximately $50,000.
- Taxes on that income will be $10,500.
- Simple math says that the above facts will yield $315 billion in revenue, very close to what the audited numbers say for 2020-2021 in the chart

above. If we continue spending at the same rate, where will the additional funds come to support the overages? Exactly, they don't exist. The government has two options:

- Option 1: Increase revenue which equates to increasing taxes (taxpayers are the primary revenue source for the federal government)
- Option 2: Borrow money from the Canadian Central Bank

For option one, an increase in revenue directly equates to a rise in taxes. Option two begs the question, where does the Canadian Central Bank get its money from? They create the money by increasing supply and then purchasing bonds which, in effect, loans money to the government. The technical term used is quantitative easing; when the government needs money to fulfill promises, they ask the central bank to print more so they can spend it. Then they use the tax dollars to pay back the principal and interest. So we ask:

- What happens when the government's debt levels are so high that they don't have enough tax revenue to pay the interest?
- What happens when interest rises as they have done rapidly over 2022?
- What happens when the cost of the national debt servicing rises sharply?

The answer: Since you can't get blood from a stone, the Canadian government continues digging deeper into more debt or raising more taxes—crippling our children and many generations to come!

Now, don't get us wrong, taxes are essential to a degree. Tax dollars fund the many valuable services Canadians benefit from in one form or another. But unfortunately, there are many things the government spends *your* money on that you don't benefit from. Hmmm, "Like what?" You ask.

In 2022, the Canadian government paid $54 million through questionable contracts with vendors that had residential addresses as their headquarters to develop the ArriveCan app, providing travelers with information on travel restrictions due to COVID-19. This app was fraught with errors and sent over 10,000 people wrongly into quarantine. When pressed for an audit, the government would not provide a list of details of how the money was spent and who received it. More importantly, an equivalent application was essentially replicated in a single weekend for less than $250,000.

Well, in 2021, included in that $628.9 billion expense number, the prime minister spent $8.6 million renovating his lakeside residence. Do you spend your family vacations there? Are you benefiting from his eight-million-dollar renovations? This is a tough spending pill to swallow when the average home price in Toronto has risen to over a million dollars. And most cannot afford a million-dollar home earning an average income of $50,000 a year—forcing more individuals to rent.

In the year 2020, there was another "misappropriation" that took place, known as the WE Charity scandal. Here, the prime minister paid $456 million, out of *our* tax dollars, to family members for event appearances. Followed by the Trudeau government sending three million dollars to the World Economic Forum, headquartered in Davos, Switzerland. And to further send $1.576 billion to the United Nations and International Organizations. So essentially, Trudeau's government sent our tax dollars—our hard-earned wealth—to fund international institutions and causes that weren't even Canadian that you will never benefit from! Therefore, your money is not only *leaving* you, but your money is also *leaving* Canada!

Think that's the worst of it? Think again. The government happily takes and spends your money, then turns around and contributes to the very cause of interest rate hikes that impact you—resulting in even more financial pressure. For example, on June 1, 2022, they increased the interest rate by 1.5%. That means it takes far more money to buy the things you need, such as a home or car because the interest rate applied to those loans is higher. The Bank of Canada has the mandate to keep the consumer price index (CPI) at 2%. Their response to rising CPI is raising interest rates. If, in June 2022, the CPI is at 8.1%, with the general consumer lending rate on mortgages around 3%, what direction will the Bank of Canada go to drive inflation down? Right, the interest rates will need to keep going up!

Now, can the government weaken the Canadian currency by printing more money? Yes, they can and have. In fact, during the lockdown period for Covid-19, the government printed five times the amount of money into existence. The more money they print, the less value is assigned to each Canadian dollar. When the currency is devalued like that, everything you buy, from food to clothes, to gas, costs more. Literally, everything you buy just to live goes up in price. The highest the Consumer Price Index went up to in 2022 was 8.1%.

And at the time of writing this book, fresh fruit was up 10%, rice was up 4%, and gas took a 60% jump in prices. Higher prices mean more money out of your pocket!

The government takes your money upfront through taxes, spends it as they wish, and then silently takes it from you by devaluing the dollars you have. It's like your wallet is in a vice and getting pressure from both ends until all your money is squeezed out.

While Canadians are focused on gambling for the next home-run investment, very few Canadians recognize the government's huge role in their ability to build and *keep* wealth. It would be silly to believe you can increase your wealth without considering the tax policies' impact on you. Now is the time to act and educate yourself on how to legally minimize your lifetime tax payments to a government that routinely misspends your hard-earned cash!

The Facts About Canadian Taxation

What is the general Canadian family burden when it comes to taxes? In 2021, there was a report created by the Fraser Institute. This annual report looked at Canadians with a household income of around $130,000, where 43% went to taxes and 35.7% went to necessities. This is a crucial tipping point: the Canadian household paid more taxes to the government than the average wage earner spent on living expenses. Albeit some of the taxes will pay for things you benefit from, some do not—as we discussed previously. So, it begs the question, are the taxes Canadians pay worth it? A higher tax bill doesn't mean higher quality service. Do municipalities shovel your driveway? Do your children get more attention from their teachers or less?

If you have a two-person household that generates $200,000, like the Fraser report indicates, often, one salary is consumed almost entirely in taxes. We have worked with many clients whose cost of living is below their annual tax bill, which is true in practice and theory. For example, here you can see the impact of taxation for a single income of $200,000 based on a resident of Ontario in the year 2022.

Source: Taxes versus the Necessities of Life: The Canadian Consumer Tax Index 2022 Edition, Fuss, Jake, Evin, Ryan (2022, September). Fraser Institute. Copyright, 2023.

Look at it from a cash flow basis. For every $100 you earn, $43 goes to some form of government. If that doesn't bother you, think about how much of your hard-earned money is simply going to waste. In addition, incomes rarely increase at the same pace as the cost of living. Imagine the price of chicken breasts increased to $27/kg. And with the Government taking $43 from every $100 you earn, how will you adequately feed your family? Exactly. Something is seriously wrong here. The government's policies are taxing you, me and our fellow Canadians into poverty.

Now, while there are some things in life and taxes you can't control, there are some you can. And I promise that we will address those in the coming chapters. But first, you need to understand the problem so the solution becomes clear. The problem is the income tax system in Canada and how it operates.

- Income tax is a tax imposed on income generated by businesses and individuals within the applicable government jurisdiction.
- Income tax is based on residency, established based on the number of days you reside in Canada and the province you're located in.
- A person who is a Canadian resident is taxed on their worldwide income, not just what they earned in Canada.
- It's a progressive system; the more you make, the more they take.
- The above tax rules are designed by the government.

This system was apparently designed to collect revenue for the government to operate for the people it serves. You can find these rules outlined in the Income Tax Act and read how they affect you. Unfortunately, the Income Tax Act is not easy to read and has transformed into a massive set of rules requiring legal and financial professionals to understand and interpret them. Even the CRA agents make mistakes interpreting the rules.

Let's look back at history. Canada joined World War I in 1914. In 1917, the Canadian government introduced the Income Tax War Act as a temporary tax against Canadians' income and increased the scope of what was deemed "business profits." Despite the war ending, the tax remained in place, and the Income Tax Act was introduced in 1948 to make it permanent. Despite Canadians being unhappy about paying these taxes, the government introduced laws and penalties to deduct taxes from the citizen's sources of income—like the bank robber, the government went to where the money was and took it.

A caveat for those who don't realize it, every time you introduce money back into the system, the system can tax you again and again. First, you earn money and taxes are levied on that income. Then, when you invest some portion of what you keep, and assuming you make money (a capital gain or income), those events trigger more taxable events. Then, when you buy goods and services, you pay taxes on those purchases. It's a never-ending cycle and you just sit there and take it. The laundry list of taxes creates a constant drag on your financial progress, and for those who have worked hard to earn and save, you get hit the hardest. Yet, we all just sit there and take it

But we must impress upon you to pay your taxes on time. Just know that if you underpay, the government will charge you penalties and interest and increase your chances of an audit; if you overpay, they will leave you alone because your error of overpaying, is not their concern. The apparent reason is the government wants your money. So, it all comes down to this:

- Pay your taxes to a lawful minimum.
- Know how to pay only the amount that you are legally obligated to.
- Ensure you don't unknowingly put yourself in a position to pay more taxes than necessary.

You will achieve the above points by collaborating with professionals who understand tax laws. The professional you choose should operate only by the letter of the law and have the experience and strategies around taxation to apply them effectively to your unique circumstances. They will be your *partner* in this endeavor, as *you* are ultimately responsible for keeping onerous taxes away from your wealth.

Summary

"Wherever your wealth resides, someone is going to try and steal it." – R. Nelson Nash

---

We suspect you've picked up our book because you have some wealth to protect and that you've worked hard for that money. We get it. We've been where you are and have worked tirelessly to find ways to keep more of the money we earn within our family. We don't mind paying our fair share of taxes (if anyone could actually pinpoint what that fair share amount actually is) for things that will benefit our families and our great country in some fashion. However, many taxpayers are increasingly concerned about the lack of direct control and accountability over government spending. It does not take long to find some questionable expenditures that may not favor Canadians.

But we must ask a logical question: **Will the government require more or less money in the future?**

Likely more, given the amount of debt accumulated. Yet, here's the thing, the more they need, the more civil unrest over taxation they could incite. And to keep that unrest in check, the government will create "exceptions to the rule" for you to shelter some of your money from taxes. The matter becomes whether you should use those exceptions or consider if even better options are available to you already.

"When taxation becomes onerous to the point where government officials sense rebellion, they always resort to exceptions to the rule."
– **R. Nelson Nash**

The government may sometimes distort rules and laws to support their taxation and spending. Just look at the civil unrest in February 2022 when Canada gained international attention using extreme measures against its peacefully protesting citizens. The government then froze millions of dollars in Canadian public banks in retaliation which we will discuss later.

"...governments fully understand they are dealing with a parasite-host relationship. The government is not capable of producing anything – it gets all its sustenance from the productive element of society. Government is a parasite and lives off the productive taxpayers, the host. It is self-evident that if the parasite takes all the produce out of the hose, then both parties die!" – R. Nelson Nash

Jayson had the good fortune of mentorship by Nelson Nash, creator of The Infinite Banking Concept®. And Nelson explained to him the importance of safeguarding your wealth this way, "Jayson, imagine you and I are in a tent in the desert, and we have everything we need to be comfortable. We have water, food, beds, air conditioning, etc. Now, Jayson doesn't look over his shoulder at the camel that just poked his head into our tent. And if he doesn't do something fast, the entire camel will end up inside of our tent. However, you need to keep the camel out of your tent."

Well, friends, we are here to tell you that the camel was a metaphor for the Canadian Revenue Agency (CRA). The CRA is the taxation arm of the government, reaching into your pockets and taking your wealth!

If you don't do something to protect your money from the government, they will tax away your wealth and spend it in ways you may not support. We don't want to see that happen. We want to explain how you can keep more wealth for your business, yourself, and your family lawfully, by using the processes and financial tools we will discuss in this book. We are here to help you "keep the camel out of your tent."

But before we dive into the information, understand that at the end of this book, you will *not* know all the nuances of taxation, nor will you want to. Our content is designed to create awareness, not turn you into a tax professional. However, what you will come away with is a solid awareness of lawful ways to protect your wealth from onerous taxation. And that knowledge may incite you to speak with the right person on our team who can assist you. At the end of this book, we will provide links to those incredible resources.

Chapter Two

Where Does Your Wealth Reside?

"Beware of little expenses. A small leak will sink a great ship."
– Benjamin Franklin

Henry:

My father fled China to escape the communist regime, ending up in Canada. This is where he met my mother. The two worked exceptionally hard to provide for our family. Working for three dollars an hour didn't go far, and my parents sacrificed greatly to ensure I wouldn't have to endure what they did.

However, as I told you in my introduction, my parents didn't discuss money because it was a source of tension. So, naturally, this impacted my views and desires for my future and, ultimately, why I became an accountant—I wanted greater control over the monies I earned. And yes, in some ways, that was a false sense of security. Because, despite my professional success, I started to question my future and became an avid reader, absorbing as much financial knowledge as possible that traditional education never covered. I began to fill in the gaps in my previous assumptions.

But in 2015, tragedy struck my family. Both my mom and dad were diagnosed with cancer—four months after I left my corporate career to become an entrepreneur—an unimaginable blow. It was as if my world had stopped spinning. Knowingly, I neglected my day-to-day life to be there for them. And life became a constant push to ensure they would conquer this death sentence. To make it happen, I sunk almost every dime I had into their treatment—something I will never regret.

However, I used that time to absorb as much information as possible on the state of the Canadian healthcare system. I uncovered that the system needs re-evaluation because it's not serving the citizens of our great country as it should.

Today, in 2022, my mother is still alive and well. My father didn't have the same outcome, unfortunately. And as my father was nearing the end, one of the most challenging tasks I undertook involved transitioning his assets. The arduous process began with me meeting with his financial advisor at one of the big banks. To say that it was an eye-opening event would be an understatement.

Learning the amount of money my father had so diligently put away in a registered retirement saving plan (RRSP) on his small salary invoked an unbelievable feeling of pride. Yet, when I recalculated the amount of money he squirreled away over 15 years into the RRSP and compared it to his account balance, the amounts were essentially equal. The shock felt like a knife to my heart. My dad, like other Canadians, was advised to invest money in an RRSP for his retirement.

For my father's specific situation, investing or "saving" into an RRSP made no sense from a tax standpoint. He was already paying the lowest taxes at 15%, so a refund wouldn't make any difference which I will explain later. If my father reached 71, he would've been forced to convert his RRSP into a registered retirement income fund (RRIF). That meant he would have been paying more taxes to get that money out from his RRSP and lose government entitled benefits like the Guaranteed Income Supplement. This supplement is a tax-free payment to those low-income earners, over the age of 65, by the government.

When I asked the advisor, "Why were there no gains? If I put the money into a simple indexed ETF, he would've made at least double the amount he has right now." But instead, Dad was advised to put the money into that same big bank fixed-income mutual fund with a historical average of 2%. To add insult to injury, the management expense ratio (MER) was 3.5%, coupled with the other opaque costs that were too complicated to unpack, so, essentially, the costs associated with the fund management were higher than Dad's gains.

It seemed as though the bank ended up making more than my father!

I remember holding back tears as I walked out of the meeting with my dad. I couldn't say a single thing. I was devastated. I was angry and disappointed in myself for not helping my dad. After all that he did for me, I wasted his years of hard work. Until his last day, when my father left this earth, he never held it against me—a testament to his unconditional love. Yet, his understanding and forgiveness never erased my pain from letting him down. This experience shaped many of my personal tenets, especially in serving my clients. It remains a constant and stark reminder that I don't want any other family to endure the same intense hurt and regret.

As time passed, I grappled with the contrast between my prior belief that the banking system would help him against the reality that they only looked out for themselves. The advisor's response still replays in my head when he said, "I treat my client's money like my family, and I want it to be safe." He wasn't lying to me. The principal was "safe," yet it allowed the bank to make more money than my father, who provided them the money in the first place! The advisor chose safety without consideration for growth. Whereas I now know you can have both with the right financial vehicle.

This is where knowledge is power; the more you understand, the more you can objectively decipher the good "expert" advice from the average to the misinformed advisor.

The most common message about an RRSP Canadians are fed is that you will "save on taxes today and get a tax break." No one ever talks about the dangers of imprisoning your money in an RRSP. Yet, the most significant threat is what happens when you take the money out. For example, my mom also earned a meager income and, like my dad, saved money in an RRSP based on the mainstream advice. Included in the tax rules are special transfer provisions that allow my dad's RRSP balance to transfer to my mom tax-free when my dad passes away. Now, because that balance is significant when my mom passes away—which none of us know when our best-before date is—the government will get 50% of that balance based on personal marginal income tax rules.

Now, if you recall, my parents paid about 15% of their income to taxes and, in their case, received a 15% refund for the amount they contributed into their RRSP. When she takes that money out now, Mom's paying at least 20% in taxes, and what's worse, is when she reaches 71, she will be forced to withdraw the minimum amount as it rolls into a registered retirement income fund (RRIF). When she withdraws the established minimum amount, not only will she pay 20% in taxes, but it will impact her other government benefits. In her specific scenario, this puts her close to anywhere around 40% in taxes. With 15% in and 40% out, how does that make any sense?

For many, receiving a tax refund upfront on their initial RRSP contributions was the dangling carrot on a stick. Now, just like my parents, years later, they are discovering that deferral has earned them very little overall in growth, and it may well cost them more in taxes and lost benefits down the road when they need it most! And this is the vehicle the government pushes you to be in for your retirement years?

Based on my experience with my parents, it seemed as though the combination of the government and the banks were getting more money from me than I was getting myself. It was here that I began my education on acquiring and protecting wealth for my family while cutting out the banks and even the government as much as legally possible from the equation. And so I took control of my investing to start, but it wasn't until I picked up a book titled, *Becoming Your Own Banker*®, when I had another epiphany.

Yes, if you've read any other book in the series with my co-authors Jayson Lowe and Richard Canfield, you already know about Nelson and his incredible process named the "Infinite Banking Concept." If you haven't, we will share some basic concepts here, but I suggest you get your hands on a copy of the Amazon #1 bestseller, *Canadian's Guide to Wealth Building Without Risk*—it's worth the read.

First, understand that whoever controls the flow of your money is the one who accumulates wealth. If you aren't directing your money flow, then someone else is, and that someone else is the one getting rich, not you. For example, when you are depositing money into the banks in the form of savings or investments, you place the banks in control over the use and motion of your money. And after reading Nelson's book, I started to see how much of my wealth was trapped in a system I had no control over.

Second, if you've listened to Jayson and Richard's podcast "Wealth Without Bay Street," you've heard Jayson comment, "Wherever wealth resides, someone will eventually try to steal it." And if you go back and re-read the first chapter or watch the news, this statement is unequivocally true!

Now, most, if not many responsible, hard-working Canadians, not unlike my mom and dad, and just like you, save money inside of an RRSP, bank, or invest money in a mutual fund, or the stock market hoping the money will grow and be preserved. Why? Because this is mainstream financial advice that we are heavily marketed to, and led to believe these are the best tools to save for our retirement. But are they? Note, we are not suggesting that any of the tools listed above are either good, bad, or otherwise. They just are, meaning each tool has its own set of characteristics in terms of control, taxation, volatility, liquidity, and so on. It will always be our view that everyone's financial circumstances, objectives and knowledge levels are unique.

The issue comes down to this. If you don't alter how you handle your wealth and where it resides, someone, namely the banks and the government, will find a way to take it from you. Mindset matters here. Yet, you can't embrace an alternative solution unless you understand the problem, and then change your actions accordingly. Where does your wealth reside? Are you in a position of total and absolute control? Is your money even growing enough to make a difference in your future? Think about all of this as we dive into the areas where most Canadians keep their money.

Where do Canadians Keep their Wealth?

Basically, most Canadians follow mainstream advice on where to store their money:

- Banks
- Stocks
- Bonds
- Mutual Funds
- Commodities, such as Gold and Silver
- RRSPS
- Or a combination of all the above

Banks

From an early age, your parents may have taught you the value of saving money for tomorrow. You may have been told, I'm sure, to put away any extra cash to prepare for retirement or the unexpected, not unlike my parents and their shocking medical diagnosis. It can and will happen to many, if not all, of us at some point. So, yes, that was good advice, preparation matters.

Then, you were most likely encouraged to deposit your money into someone else's bank to earn interest. Again, not poor advice on the surface. Except, over the last 30 years, the amount of interest a bank pays is minuscule at best. And whatever you do earn in interest each year, that interest becomes taxable, and so the government will take a portion. With every deposit, a conventional bank is able to lend even more money into existence, and the owners of that bank (the stockholders) have an expectation of profit, and they want it in the form of dividends. In exchange for your deposits, the conventional bank pays you interest which nowhere near amounts to the profits the bank generates overall. You only get a portion of the returns that can be generated. How does that make you feel?

To solidify this point, let me say this differently. When you deposit your money in a conventional bank, you become an unsecured creditor of that bank, meaning you are lending money to a bank with no collateral—and that places you at the bottom of the totem pole if the bank were to experience insolvency or a run on the bank. The bank pays you pitiful interest and lends more money into existence *with* collateral to earn interest significantly higher than what they pay. They're profiting massively off the money you freely leave with them. To add insult to injury, they charge you ridiculous fees to handle *your* own money within their institution. Let me repeat this: Banks charge *you* to make money on *your* money! They'll charge you for anything you do with your money, such as a wire transfer. Add to that the consistent increase of such fees, which should have you asking: Has the quality of service also increased along with these bank charges? I'll let you ponder that for yourself.

Life happens to all of us. You may get sick, you may want to buy a home, or your kid(s) may need to go to college, and you'll need ready access to money to make it happen. Suppose you decide to take a loan out so you don't touch your "nest egg," or maybe you don't have enough cash in the bank. That same bank you warehouse your money in, or one just like it, will have you jump through several pre-qualification hoops to prove you can pay the loan back. And if you are lucky enough to qualify, the lender dicates the repayment schedule, interest rates, and terms. Hence the phrase, whoever has the gold makes all the rules. Can you recall a time in your life, when presented with the terms of a loan, caused anxiety or stress? The lender's mandate is to charge more interest on loans than they pay on deposits.

Think of it this way: Individuals who lend money to other Individuals, would understandably want a return of interest that exceeds their cost of capital, because their money is tied up. To the contrary, however, Canadians leave their hard-earned money on deposit with *someone else's* bank (essentially a low interest loan), receive practically nothing in return, and pay a variety of fees. Reflect on that for a moment. Doesn't it seem like the banking business is a great business to be in? How much better could your life be financially if you could take a page from the bank's playbook and control that function as it relates to your own needs?

Stocks, Bonds, Mutual Funds, or Commodities

Every financial product has its own set of characteristics in terms of:

- Access
- Control

- Guarantees
- Taxation
- Volatility
- Risk
- Liquidity

When you hand control of your money over to someone else who thinks they can do better with it than you can, you're at a disadvantage when compared to someone who's in a position of total and absolute control. Markets rise, markets fall, and you have zero control. Yet, while that phenomenon continues, the process of banking goes on no matter what. Any financial product subjected to volatility or market manipulation is a polite description of gambling. Yes, one could accumulate a lot of account value in a bull market, but that accumulation is not real until it is turned into money. What you think is there, isn't really there. It's just an illusion. And when the market drops, and your stocks, or mutual funds, take a nosedive, the mainstream financial sector will repeat, "Don't panic. The market will come back!" Perhaps this is true, but your follow-up question should be, "On who's schedule?" Important to note that if your investment account(s) are subjected to fees like management expense ratios (MERs), the institution receives recurring fees on your entire account value, not just the gains. And the institution makes money whether you win or lose.

For example, your account value rises steadily during a "bull" market, and you're all set to retire with a big nest egg. Suddenly the market turns for the worse. The economy takes a downturn, taxes go up, and your stock portfolio is dropping substantially in value. Has this ever happened to you? Go back to 2008, 2009. Back then, many individuals watched their life savings evaporate as the financial crisis unfolded. And they could no longer afford to retire anymore. At the time this book was written, there was uncertainty in the economy, inflation and interest rates were both rising, and the purchasing power of a dollar was severely diminished. For hard-working families, their financial plans are derailed, and for those on a fixed income, like retirees, it's a recipe for increased stress and anxiety, precisely when it's needed the least. Combine that with the 2022 market meltdown, throw in some geo-political turmoil and the idea of certainty in retirement may be out of reach.

Don't forget about the myriad of rules and restrictions at the financial institution level and those also imposed by the governing body that regulates tax-qualified plans, such as registered retirement savings accounts. Depending on the combination of the account type (pension, LIRA, RRSP, RESP etc) and then the investment vehicle, this could include withdrawal fees, transfer fees, management fees, withholding taxes and even worse are restrictions regarding access to your funds. Don't forget, when it comes to registered accounts such as RRPS and pensions, someone else makes the rules and if those rules change for the worse, you have no control over it.

Have you ever asked yourself why banks and advisors want you to "keep" your money in *their* institutions? The answer may be obvious. If you withdraw your money, the bank would have less money to multiply for the benefit of their stockholders and borrowers, less management fees, management expense ratios, transaction commissions, and more. The banking business is remarkably profitable. And someone must perform the banking function as it relates to your needs. That someone *can* and should be *you*.

A few remarks about Registered Retirement Savings Plans

Registered retirement savings plans. Are they worth it? We are told, "Work hard and save for your retirement utilizing the RRSP program created by the Canadian government." Money deposited into an RRSP is typically invested in mutual funds, money market funds, equities, etc. And the moment the account is created, you're on the government's radar because you file a tax return each year and your account is "registered." But the tax benefits are amazing aren't they? If we're referring to the deferral of taxes, maybe not. You're not only deferring the payment of tax, you're also deferring the calculation, meaning the amount actually due at a future date when you need access to your money. And the larger your account balance becomes, the larger the tax problem.

Do you know what the tax rates will be in the future? We don't and neither does anyone else. That creates uncertainty and uncertainty is no way to plan. Logical questions to ask are: "Will our government likely require more or less money in the future? And where will that money come from?"

And just like I discovered when I checked on my own Father's RRSP, there may not be as much money there as you think. If you have an RRSP, when you review your account value (i.e. $500,000), a portion of that account value is not yours, meaning, if we factored in a 30% withholding rate, $150,000 of that account value belongs to the Canada Revenue Agency. And, to make matters worse, you're paying fees on the *entire* $500,000 account value, not only the $350,000 amount that is actually yours. Also important to note that withholding tax is *not* based on income. It's based on withdrawal amounts. And inflation only amplifies the problem.

You see, when you withdraw money out of your RRSP's, a withholding tax is triggered and the percentage (%) is based on each withdrawal amount. For example, you request a withdrawal from your RRSP of $100,000. The institution where your account resides withholds thirty (30) percent (%) or $30,000 and forwards that to the Canada Revenue Agency. CRA waits for you to file your next income tax return. You receive $70,000. The entire amount withdrawn, $100,000, is added to your next tax return as income and you receive credit for the $30,000 already withheld. Depending upon your total income for that year, you could easily end up owing even more in taxes. Who's in a position of total control? It's certainly not you. How does that make you feel? Therefore, if you have taxable accounts, you have a problem, and so do your beneficiaries. You have to reckon with an absence of control, uncertainty, and eventually the deemed disposition rule, which we will discuss later on.

Consider financial institutions reporting every RRSP contribution and account balance in the nation to the government. Now, just imagine government institutions rubbing their hands together and salivating over all of those future tax revenues. All of the hard-earned money their fellow Canadians accumulated inside a tracked financial instrument that they dictate the rules on.

For clarity, we are not suggesting that RRSP's are good, bad or otherwise. They just are. And like our late mentor R. Nelson Nash often said "When you understand what's going on, you'll know what to do." Financial products that have an absence of control, no guarantees, access with penalties, and volatility are far less attractive when compared to a financial product that possesses attributes to the contrary.

A fact worth thinking about: In our fifteen years of practice, we've never met a single person who's attributed the wealth they've accumulated to RRSP's.

"If the minority of people in the world are accumulating and controlling the wealth, why do we continue to do what the majority do financially?" – **Garret Gunderson**

Let's take a step back for a moment and review a few definitions.

The definition of a *system* is "a regularly interacting or interdependent group of items forming a unified whole." There are two very notable systems to look at: The income tax system and the banking system. Now, as we analyze these, we've also got to critically assess the designs of these systems, especially in comparative perspectives with how they interact with you.

We've described much about the income tax system earlier, stating it is a legal form of deductions or payments to the government from its citizens, you. These payments are revenue to the government with the supposition that money is used to benefit Canada as a whole—the government collects and spends your money, often without your approval on what and how much it's spent on. Now, if the revenue can't support the expenditures, the government is forced to borrow from the central bank. We already know that you must borrow if you spend more than you make and have no capital saved. When you borrow, there's interest payable on the principal amount borrowed. So, here's a question for you to ponder: If there is not enough revenue to pay for the spending, then how will the government pay the principal and interest back? Where does the government get more money from? As we've clearly indicated, it must come from taxable sources of personal income and business revenues. As we write this book, the government has introduced a new luxury vehicle tax, increased carbon taxes, and instituted an empty home tax on Canadians. The government has also raised contribution rates to the Canadian Pension Plan (CPP) and employment insurance (EI). All are resulting in more of your hard-earned money flowing away from you.

To learn more about this, access our bonus video content at **keeptaxesaway.com.**

The next system is the banking system. The Bank Act was passed by Parliament to regulate Canada's chartered banks. The Bank of Canada operates as an arm of the federal government to carry out its monetary policy, acting as a lender of last resort to chartered banks. It holds the deposits of governments and chartered banks and then issues notes or money as needed. The Bank Act allows for chartered banks to engage in what is called "fractional reserve banking." This means only a fraction of bank deposits are backed by cash on hand and available for withdrawal. Now, consider that for a moment. The Bank Act allows the banks to decide their own reserves.

For example, you deposit $5,000 into a conventional bank. That bank may choose to hold ten percent ($500) in its own reserve account with the central bank. The moment that $5,000 deposit lands on the books, the bank can lend more money into existence. In exchange for your deposit, the bank issues an "IOU" or "on demand deposit," meaning you can demand some or all of your deposit back at your convenience. Because banks can lend money into existence—provided they have depositors leaving money there—it's no surprise the banks want your funds. They operate on the theory that not everyone will come running to the banks to get their money back simultaneously, known as "a run on the banks." So, we ask you: What could go wrong? Remember, as we mentioned earlier, what you think is there isn't really there. It is an illusion.

Everything begins with mindset, the way humans think. And so, let's "think" about the traditional banking system inside a construct of four characters in a financial play:

- Depositor – places money in the bank for safekeeping, earns some interest
- Borrower – accesses someone else's money in the form of a loan, then repays interest + principle
- Banker – this person sets out the rules such as access, interest, terms, qualification criteria, and approvals
- Bank owner – the one character who makes the most money (understandably so) in this cast

The depositor and borrower cover the overwhelming majority of Canadians. This same group is unaware that when you put your money into the banking system, the banker sets the rules on what you can borrow and how much the bank profits from each transaction. They also don't realize that without the depositor there is nothing to lend and the banker is out of a job, while the bank owner would have to close up shop and may even go bankrupt. The depositor enables the lender to lend and the borrower is the one character who makes this entire play possible.

You can, and *should* become all four characters in the financial play.

So, here's something that I want to highlight. The more you feed your money into this system, the more power you give to the bank owner to make more profit. The greater the profits they make, the greater they expand. Then low-and-behold, you see branches everywhere duplicating the same successful formula, exponentially growing their profit margins. If they have branches, rest assured that they've effectively built a massive infrastructure scaling their profitable formula. The larger and stronger they get, the more individuals rely on them. And the more people like yourself rely on the banking system, the more outlandish fees they get to charge you. And yes, it's all legal, thanks to The Bank Act.

Remember that someone must perform the function of banking as it relates to your needs. That someone *can*, and *should* be *you*. And what we are alluding to is a process.

How would you feel if the bankers were out of your life? Some say it's amazing. Others say it's a peaceful, stress-free way of life.

Let us tell you about a client we have, whom we will refer to as Chris, and who we will reference throughout the remainder of the book to outline key points. Chris was an attendee at one of our events. And when he turned age 47, Chris booked a meeting with Henry to complete a financial "x-ray" of his situation:

- Chris is a mechanical engineer.
- He earns $150,000 a year. In actuality, he only *handles* $150K per year.
- He is self-employed.
- He saves $25,000 yearly inside of an RRSP, and $250,000 has been piled up in the account to date.

When Henry sat back, he asked Chris, "What are you looking to do?"

"Well, I went to one of your financial education events and decided to begin building up accessible funds in order to do some real estate investing. I want to create more passive income. I don't think I will be able to retire on what I have inside of my RRSP. My goal when I retire is to have $65,000 of after tax cash flow per year."

Henry shared with Chris that if he kept going on the same path, he would not achieve his goal, identifying a few important issues:

- Chris was paying way too much in taxes. Money out the window that he will never get back.
- Chris was struggling to get by daily.
- There were no accessible funds to use for investing.
- Chris most likely wouldn't be able to retire at 65.

Can you, or someone you know identify with Chris? And when you were younger, in college, for example, and you aspired to make $150,000 a year, did you anticipate you would struggle? Probably not. But the sad truth is that many people do end up struggling.

Why? Because most follow the mainstream financial advice and place all of their money inside financial products that limit their control as described above. People allow others to control the use and the motion of their money. We believe that financial control should be in your hands, not the banks, not the government, and not some temperamental market. That is why we show our clients how to keep more taxes away from their wealth.

Essentially, Chris needed less income taxed, more money flowing into a financial vehicle to grow his wealth tax-free, and have ready access to money for life's expenses. Did Henry get him there? You bet. Did Henry help Chris understand and then utilize a financial product as the tool to get the job done? He sure did. And in the coming chapters, we will explain the steps Henry and Chris took.

Summary

"Risk comes from not knowing what you're doing."
— **Warren Buffett**

In truth, most of us do what we know. We follow the pre-established guidelines set by previous generations. We go to school to setup a good career, we buy a home, try to pay cash for things if possible, hopefully pay down our debts so we can save for retirement, and squirrel away some dollars for unexpected surprises. But let's face it, when it comes to handling our money, we return to what was done before. And in doing so, we often repeat mistakes that we've made in the past or repeat those made by our parents before us.

Our financial coaches encourage you to continue successful behaviors in your best interest, such as saving, investing, and safeguarding the assets that strategically align for you. But to increase your efficiency, you should consider altering your process or the *how*, as we like to call it. Clearly, not all financial vehicles are the same, and although some might benefit you in one way, they may harm you in others. Taking a holistic approach, we will show you what works and what doesn't, ultimately identifying the one vehicle that can give you the ultimate flexibility, control, accumulation, and safety you need. And that vehicle is a dividend-paying participating whole life insurance policy (or system of policies), ideally with a mutual life insurance company which will be explained later.

Chapter Three

First Four of Five Steps to Keeping Taxes at Bay

"The hardest thing in the world to understand is the income tax."
– **Albert Einstein**

You go to work, like our client Chris in the previous chapter, and you earn a decent salary, but most of it goes to paying taxes, covering basic living costs, and some you manage to scrape off the top to save for retirement or the unexpected. But *where* you accumulate that "nest egg" matters. As we've stated repeatedly, wherever wealth resides, others will try to steal it, like the government, through onerous taxation.

Remember how, based on Henry's initial assessment of our client Chris's finances, he determined that Chris was paying far too much in taxes unnecessarily? Well, if we were to wager a guess, so are you. For every dollar the government siphons out of your pocket, that's one less dollar you can deploy into something else that will multiply more money for you.

And the government is always thinking of new ways to tax more of what you accumulate. For example, in the most recent federal budget release, the government communicated they want to investigate your RRSP's. Why do you think that is? Logically, (although unsubstantiated), that may have something to do with taxes. Imagine what they could possibly want to know. Perhaps they want more clarity on what tax dollars are available to them (today or in the future) for the mounting national debt problem we discussed earlier. Logically, yes! If you recall, back in 2016, the Canadian Revenue Agency (CRA) required you to disclose your principal residence. Why? Again, they want to know more about what you have. This gives them the data to model future potential tax changes, including wealth transfers, providing a clear view to future additions to tax revenues.

Since all your information is spread among multiple databases, the act of information consolidation allows the CRA clear visibility. Then they can assess which "levers" they can pull to extract more of *your* money. And the owners of this data will have tremendous power over you. We've already seen levels of encroachment through implied consent. This simple request is an initial indicator of the government potentially creeping into the tax exemption rule that applies to your principal residence or changing the current exemption on capital gains from 50% to 75%. One should assume that the more information they get on you, the more they have to work with in terms of future taxation changes. To reiterate: Data centralization works for the government, not you.

That said, we have to ask: Other than complaining about the amount of taxes taken from your paycheck or any additional amounts owed at the end of the year, when do you think about taxes? Most of us try not to think about them because it's painful. We get it. However, the issue is you need to always think about them in terms of building wealth. Taxes can represent a large portion of your wealth permanently flowing away from you. And in the upcoming discussion on methods to deal with reducing your tax bill, they require planning. This is not in the form of being reactive, where you file your taxes by their deadlines and receive an additional refund, but a forward-thinking process for multiple years and even across future generations. So prepare to start changing things now, to be ready when the tax collector comes knocking.

Let's discuss how to keep the tax collector away from your money. Again, we are not describing tax evasion or deliberate non-payment of taxes. To the contrary, what we will describe is not only lawful, it's also been in existence since 1847, long before the Income Tax Act came to be.

How does one approach this? Well, our method involves what we call the five "D's" of *defense against taxation*. It will be your personal "pentagon of defense" for your wealth, protecting you against having too much of your income confiscated by the government in the form of onerous taxation:

- Deferring Income
- Defining Income
- Designing Income
- Dividing Income
- ?

Note we've deliberately left out the 5th D because of its importance; it demands its own chapter.

Given the complexity of the Income Tax Act, where new rules have been added incrementally over time, you will need to combine the various defense strategies. Often, you will need to employ multiple "defenses," depending on your situation, to maximize the legally allowable tax savings and mitigation. These above-listed methods are universally applicable irrespective of the taxable legal entity—corporate or personal. However, I must emphasize that these concepts should not be applied without the designated guidance of a tax professional. There are many technicalities and nuances the average Canadian may not be aware of, and if incorrectly used, it could land you in very troubled waters. These strategies are meant to provide you with a roadmap to guide your conversation with your tax professional, who understands your unique parameters and objectives and how they will fit with the underlying technical rules or if they exist at all for you.

As we continue, it's worth repeating that our goal is to educate broadly on a highly complex set of income tax rules. Again, the goal is not to transform you into a tax expert but to make you aware of any potential leaks you have so you can take action on assessing your situation with and only with a knowledgeable tax professional.

Deferred Taxes

Deferring taxes allows you to take portions of your current taxable income and pay taxes on it later based on where you've placed it. When we say "where you placed it," we refer to the financial and governmental institutions and their corresponding vehicles—the RRSP, mutual funds, and so forth.

Where your money is stored can define something as taxable income now or later. So, if you've put it in a tax-deferred vehicle, such as an RRSP, the money remains nontaxable until it's withdrawn. Therefore, in theory, the expectation is that you will use this vehicle to save for retirement. The assumption is when you remove those funds, you will be older, possibly no longer earning an income, and if so, you will fall into a lower tax bracket paying a lower tax rate on that money. This is a put-off-to-tomorrow scenario that is promoted to work in your favor today and hopefully down the road. Effectively, it can temporarily reduce your tax burden in a year when you have a higher income from windfalls.

Let's suppose you get a bonus this year. Sounds good, right? Well, not so fast. That bonus will likely cost you more because you will have to pay more taxes and not proportionally. The bonus amount bumps you into a higher bracket, and the tax rate applied will be higher; therefore, the cost could be even higher. However, as a strategy, if you placed that bonus into a deferred tax vehicle, such as an RRSP, then you temporarily mitigate that from your current income tax bill calculation.

The point of tax deferral is to remove the concentration of income from one year to a future year. This can be achieved by receiving a smaller portion over time and/or changing the way you receive those monies in the future to avoid triggering a higher income tax bracket.

However, the downside of deferred taxable income depends on when you must withdraw the funds. Most Canadians have busy lives and often forget about the money they put in and therefore do not have an RRSP "meltdown" strategy. Every time your money sits in a tax-deferred mechanism, you expose yourself to an increase in future income taxes and concentrated deemed disposition tax (more on that later in the bonus chapter). If your tax rate is much higher upon removal, the perceived benefit ceases to exist or worsens. Therefore, deferring taxes using this method is situationally specific, but it can work well in the ordinary course of life. It falls apart, however, if you remove the money too early or your tax rate is higher than when you exercised the deferral.

Defining Income

How you "label" your income sources will attract different tax rules. This creates a spectrum of taxable income ranging from least to most.

I'll separate the definitions into two main categories, active and passive.

Active income can be directly linked to your production. The income you generate from your work (production) is generally taxed at the highest rates.

The income that produces the highest taxes is employment income that's reported on the T4. Very few rules exist allowing T4 employees to deduct expenses for generating revenue (e.g., the gas you pay to drive to your employer).

The next would be the middle income, which is business income, which falls into corporate and self-employment income.

In the case of business income, generally, as long as these expenses were incurred in support of your earning income, you can use some living expenses to reduce the taxable amount, such as cell phone or internet. But again, this rule has many nuances. We recommend sitting down with a tax professional to ensure accuracy in applying the tax laws to assess whether it was incurred during earning business. There are many distinctions, like golf fees, where you may have paid for golf fees for doing business. Still, the CRA specifically disallows deducting golf fees as expenses for generating income.

Passive income can be directly linked to income generated from your possessions, such as stocks, bonds, real estate, collectables, bullion, etc. They are taxed in common categories such as capital gains, dividends, and interest.

Currently, capital gains are only 50% taxable. For example, suppose you paid $80,000 for some stocks and sold those stocks later for $100,000. Your capital gain is $20,000, but $10,000 (50%) is taxable, which would be included in your income for that tax year. As a unique feature of capital gains, any capital losses accumulated in the past can be applied against future gains.

Based on the activities in how you earn the income, you need to be careful. For example, if you sell an investment property in which you intended to be a "buy and hold," it's generally taxed as a capital gains rate because it's infrequent—that extra gain you received is not because of your production. However, if you're a serial "house-flipper," your gains are now considered business income because you are actively looking for deals. The CRA would look to push you into active business income from your production.

Did you know one unique advantage of capital gains is that you receive all the money on your gain before any tax comes off? It is only at the filing of your taxes for that year that the gain is declared and then tax payable. This gives you the advantage of working with the gross earnings before the tax bill is due. This also creates a problem for many. If you do not prepare for the tax bill because you have re-allocated the funds, you may not have liquidity for the eventual tax that must be paid. Some might even be forced to borrow from the commercial banking system to solve the tax problem.

The ability to redefine your income based on taxation rules can provide some benefits. For example, suppose someone owned a business. Instead of receiving the money in the form of a salary, they receive the money in the form of a dividend, which, all-encompassing, generally may be taxed at a lower rate. This redefinition is among the most widely discussed topics between business owners and tax professionals, so it's essential to evaluate their perspectives. This is a prime example of combining "design" and "definition" when the situation allows for it, where the corporate business owner can decide the income they want to receive.

Finally, the least of the tax spectrum is dividend income. Now when we talk about dividend income, there are three specific types:

- Eligible dividends
- Ineligible dividends
- Capital dividends

Eligible dividends get the most favorable tax treatment. These are dividends received from corporations paying higher corporate tax rates in which they pay you dividends. The most typical place you would see this is if you own public company shares in an unregistered account.

Ineligible dividends are generally what most private Canadian corporations pay. They have an advantageous tax treatment.

And capital dividends are not taxable—these arise exclusively in a corporation and generally come from the nontaxable portion of a gain of sale on a property and life insurance proceeds. This is a potent and underutilized mechanism that few professionals know how to use and plays a critical role in passing wealth to your predecessors. At Ascendant Financial, we focus on this with our team of coaches. I'll explain more of this in later chapters.

When it comes to corporations—this goes without saying that the rules of income earned inside of the corporation are very similar; however, their treatments can be much more complex with more rules, and this should definitely be discussed in detail with a tax professional.

On a personal front, the government typically has more favorable rules for passive incomes but less favorable rules for active incomes.

On a corporate front, the government has more favorable rules for active incomes but imposes much more stringent restrictions on passive income, including taxing general rental incomes at approximately 50%!

Again, this is situationally dependent. When you build the right team around yourself, you can collaborate to determine the best classifications for your income based on your situation, goals, and objective parameters.

Designing Income

Basically, this addresses how you receive your income in the taxable legal entities, impacting the amount of taxes you pay. For example, the income you receive as an employee would be as a T4. Because as we stated earlier, the income you receive from a T4 gets the most taxes. Therefore, depending on your circumstances, such as contractual, multiple clients, or business-oriented, if possible, you could move your income salary away from a highly taxable personal active form, to a more efficient structure, like corporate or business income, where the tax rates are generally lower and vice versa for passive incomes.

If successful at designing your income and shifting to a corporate structure, the first "D", deferring, can be activated to some degree without the use of an RRSP with better control in your hands vs. the RRSP, which is more control in the Government's hands, rather than yours. It does not create a deduction in the corporation but controlling how you are paid allows you to defer personal income taxes to a more strategic future year while you grow your capital base in the corporate realm.

This is where it becomes almost an art. Some of the most talented tax professionals get compensated very well for customizing tax structure designs and creating excellent frameworks for the movement of capital.

Dividing Income

Remember, the Canadian tax system is progressive, meaning the more you make, the more taxes you pay. So instead of concentrating the income into one individual/entity, dividing the income refers to spreading taxable monies across other entities wherever possible. By entities, we mean spouses, children, corporate entities, and so on.

However, I caution you here. The liberal government severely closed many opportunities for this in 2017, known as the Tax on Split Income (TOSI). For example, having a husband and wife owning a company 50/50 (Design), the wife and husband must prove a "reasonable house of work" to implement this split (Divide).

Summary

"The best things in life are free, but sooner or later the government will find a way to tax them." – **Anonymous**

At the end of any given workday, do you head home, fly through the door, and start calculating the money you earned, how much will remain with you, and how much the government will take? No, probably not. We tend to think about taxes most during tax season, right? However, given what you've learned, we must ask: When *should* you be thinking about taxes?

If you are employed, you're constantly handling money. Unfortunately, not all of it will remain with you, so you should be smart about what you do with that hard-earned cash to protect the maximum amount possible from being taken from you, namely in the form of onerous taxation. And some of the items discussed earlier in this chapter can be effective tax management strategies depending on your circumstances. However, you can't implement those ideas on the fly in your accountant's office just hours before a tax filing deadline. We must emphasize that preparation for the tax season is critical.

In our next chapter, we will explain the financial vehicle and process that will not only enable you to grow your wealth but shield it from government coffers. Using this tool will, however, require an adjustment to your thinking. It will require some upfront thought and a complete change in where you store your money. And it will be worth it because, in the end, it will eliminate that feeling of dread, and replace it with the feeling of certainty.

Chapter Four

The Fifth D and Why it's Critical for Preserving, Building, Multiplying, and Transferring Wealth

---

"Nelson Nash said, 'Remember, there's only one pool of money in the world.' And what Nelson saw was that he was pumping money into that pool the wrong way, – and it was flowing away from him instead of toward him." – Henry Wong

---

Many protested in February of 2022 during the pandemic when Canadian truckers were told to vaccinate or couldn't haul their load across the border. Yes, the protest was partly from this mandate, but many speculate it was due to growing frustration over the many restrictions Canada had imposed on its citizens in the previous 2 years. However, no matter the reason, these truckers blockaded the streets of Ottawa in a peaceful protest.

This has many controversies depending on the news source you use to get your information. Yet, no one from the Canadian government spoke to the underlying frustration among these protestors.

According to the Canadian charter, its citizens have the right to free speech and peacefully assemble. However, Justin Trudeau invoked for the first time in history, the Emergencies Act. This act, which can only be used under extremely dire circumstances, had never been used on its citizens in the country's history. Trudeau's decision made global headlines and sparked international condemnation and shame in Canada. Many wonder if the threshold to activate the Emergencies Act met the threshold for "dire circumstances."

Our intent in highlighting this situation is not to impart any political views but to acknowledge the government's power to freeze both the protestors' bank accounts and those who donated, thanks to the help of the banks. For example, some individuals with a small donation of $20 had their bank accounts frozen for weeks! This potentially left individuals and families unable to pay bills and buy food or vital medications. First, it begs the question of fair and just treatment. But secondly, it must beg the question: If the government and banks can freeze your money at will, overstepping legal boundaries, why allow your money to reside inside the banking system? This sparked a huge wake-up call for many Canadians. Who really was in control if the government could deny access to their hard-earned funds? It isn't them.

Let this fact sink in: Your money must reside somewhere!

Because of how everything is intertwined and how you've interacted with the banking and government systems, gradually seceding yourself from the system is possible. It's a change in process, mindset, and awareness that is meant to be achieved over a period of time.

Why you would consider seceding from the System

This brings us to the fifth and final 'D' of the 5 D's in our pentagon of defense to reduce taxes you owe now and into the future to protect your wealth from being taxed away from the government. That 'D' is *disconnect*.

Yes, you must disconnect from heavily relying upon someone else's system and start creating your own family banking system by implementing the process of being your own banker. Discover that you can control your life and financial destiny. Instead of leaving it in an unsecured, fee and tax-laden, up-and-down unguaranteed environment, why not move it into a safe, secure, private, and contractually guaranteed environment?

"Those who have the gold, make all the rules." – R. Nelson Nash

---

You're probably thinking, "Okay, yes, this sounds great in theory, but how does this work for me, and what does it even look like for me? This is why I want to encourage you to reach out to us—we don't design cookie cutter solutions—we meticulously engage in detailed discussions with you to create personalized family banking systems to align with your family banking needs. Our processes are centered around helping you reach your goals.

If we talk about changing the strategic location of where you're directing your money flow and storing it, we are talking about protecting your wealth. You need to start building your "warehouse of wealth" and "family banking system."

You can't expect your CPA or tax specialist to know about dividend-paying participating whole life insurance. You also can't expect your life insurance advisor to know The Infinite Banking Concept®, the process of Becoming Your Own Banker®. Every professional has their own area of specialization, defined by their experience, designation, and mission.

While we describe the use of a dividend-paying participating whole life insurance policy, for the purposes of our discussion, that's just the best tool to get the job done. And as our late mentor Nelson Nash often said "If you put the best tool to get the job done in the hands of an incompetent, not only will he not turn out any good work with the tool, he will likely break the darn tool."

Any life licensed advisor should be able to illustrate a life insurance policy. An authorized Infinite Banking practitioner on the other hand, has amassed a very specialized skillset and knowledge that other industry professionals have likely not. We see a variety of client situations with various goals and objectives daily. Our core DNA is to design your warehouse of wealth and coach you to utilize your own family banking system.

When building your warehouse of wealth, you should apply a very rigorous process to ensure that much of the money flowing through your hands is stored in this warehouse. Where possible, with training, practice and the right mindset you can keep this money circulating within your own personal economy and positively impact your family for generations.

In our view, there's really no comparison. As one of Nelson's six golden rules is to "rethink your thinking." We're not here to impose any of that on you other than letting you know the choice is yours.

Not everyone will carry the same views or goals. It's like asking, should my house have three bedrooms or four bedrooms? Two bathrooms or seven bathrooms? Open concept kitchen or closed concept? The answer to all those questions is that it all depends on a combination of what you desire and fundamentally need for your family scenario. What's important is that we sit down and have that open discussion on learning about each other and whether we're even a fit to work together.

wealthwithoutbaystreet.com/15mincall

One extreme could still be a significant dependency on someone else's banking system. The other extreme is eliminating the bankers from their life and just using someone else's bank for the convenience of debit.

Imagine changing the flow of your money away from the public banking system, whereby you cut out the middlemen (bankers and the tax collector) and redirect the flow of your money into your own family banking system. This opens the door to creating a peaceful, stress-free way of life financially. Isn't that good?

Despite the initial fear of change, I know, and by now you should know the time has come to control the function of banking as it relates to your needs and to keep taxes away from your wealth.

So, anyone who has read Jayson and Richard's book, *Canadian's Guide to Wealth Building Without Risk*, can launch an educated guess at what we are about to say. However, to disconnect from the ties that bind you to the banking system, there is a proven tool—used by hundreds of thousands of Canadians—to effectively serve you. Yes, we are talking about the participating dividend-paying whole-life policy, preferably with a mutual life insurance company.

Now, before we discuss the ins and outs of what a participating whole life policy does for you, you must understand the objective here is to implement a process and that is to create your own banking system, a process Nelson Nash called, "The Infinite Banking Concept®." And the best tool to get that job done is a flexible, high-cash value, participating whole life policy, or ideally a system of policies. However, these policies should be acquired through a mutual life insurance company. Why? Because a mutual life insurance company is what the name suggests, it is an insurance company for which, upon purchasing a policy, you become a co-owner of that company and there are no stockholders to share the profits with.

Why is this vital? If you are an owner of anything, the strategic alignment of resources is focused on the owner (you). This includes features such as a share in the profits, right? So, the same goes here where you are entitled to receive dividends annually when declared on your "participating" whole life policy—participating signifies you will receive dividends when declared. In contrast, with a stock-owned insurance company, stock owners, not policy owners, are always first in line, and receive the lion's share of attention and resources focused on keeping them happy.

So, how is this tool utilized to get the job done? All of your money is presently flowing through the books of someone else's bank. We'll say that again, someone else's bank. Hence, you are already practicing the process of banking through saving, taking out loans, repaying loans, and debiting to pay for your life's expenses. When you send all your money to someone else's bank, you empower them to make the profits, which they don't share with you. In return, the larger their infrastructure is, the more you depend on their infrastructure, that is when they monopolize their position, and can charge what they want without your consideration.

But when we talk about creating your own family banking system, we primarily speak about a place to store your money, and then from that place, control *how* you go about financing the things you need and investments that you'll purchase throughout a lifetime.

Let us be absolutely clear: When we talk about "your family banking system," it may be one policy or ideally, a system of multiple policies. The critical element here is assembling a system of policies under your whole family umbrella so that you as a family can pool all your resources together cohesively. This is contrary to conventional advice out there where everyone has their bank account and individualizes doing everything on their own which simply means using the banking system's infrastructure. Embracing the process and controlling it as it relates to your needs also creates a huge advantage in efficient wealth transfers that keep hard-earned capital where it belongs, within your family.

When you purchase a participating whole life policy, provided the associated death benefit has merit, and combined with your goals and objectives as defined by your own life aspirations, you and your coach will determine an annual premium that works for you. It must be comfortable and affordable. So instead of depositing money into someone else's banking system, you change the location of where your own money resides.

The total maximum premium consists of two separate components:

1. Required base premium
2. Optional premium

Both components have a defined purpose.

Now, the life insurance company is contractually bound to grow cash value on a daily basis which must equal the total death benefit by age 100 of the life insured. With proper policy design, and policy owner behavior, the total death benefit will increase with every premium and dividend paid, obligating the life insurance company to accelerate the growth of total cash value. Based on that information, let's focus on the total cash value because that is the equity built up inside the policy that you can borrow against to a maximum of 90% on demand, and on your terms.

For example, suppose you've been saving up money inside someone else's bank for the purpose of buying a new car. You've driven yours until the wheels fell off and it's time to replace it. Because you were so diligent in saving, the minute you paid off your current vehicle, you now have enough cash in your bank account to buy that new car. So, you go to the bank, withdraw the money out of your account, and pay for your new car in cash. Sounds good right? Yes and no.

Yes, because you aren't incurring more debt, but no, because now you've permanently transferred all of your money to someone else, never to be seen again. You can't earn any more interest on that money because you transferred that future earning power to someone else. However, if you had used a participating whole life policy to accumulate that same cash, you could access a policy loan without withdrawing or interrupting the daily growth of your own total cash value. No money leaves your policy or your control.

A policy loan is nothing like a bank loan.

Here is what we mean:

- You, the policy owner, contact the life insurance company that you co-own. You request a policy loan for a specified amount. It is a private loan between you and the life insurance company. Since it is a private loan and you are not accessing available credit from the conventional banking system, this transaction does not appear on any credit report. When requesting this policy loan, there is no qualifying, no income verification, and no repayment schedule. The money is yours to access and to use as you decide (in this example, to purchase a car).

- The total cash value in your policy remains one hundred percent (100%) intact and growing daily because it serves as collateral for the loan, AND because the life insurance company cannot interrupt the contractual guarantee of your total cash value matching your total death benefit by age 100.

- You can repay the policy loan back on your schedule and with no restrictions. Simple interest accrues on any unpaid balance and then adds to the loan on each annual policy anniversary date. You are borrowing from a financial entity that you co-own with other Canadians and they share their profits with you, year over year, in the form of dividends and policy owner's equity.

- Your total cash value balance will continue to experience uninterrupted daily growth.

- If you died with a policy loan balance outstanding, then the amount owed is deducted from the total death benefit before the balance of the death benefit proceeds are paid to your named beneficiaries income tax free. But as long as you are alive, we always recommend repaying your policy loans so you can re-access the capital over and over again for all the things you need to finance throughout your lifetime.

This is how you can systematically, with multiple policies, control the banking function as it relates to your needs and fund all those things that you need in life, like cars, homes, appliances, education, business equipment, or a business. Some of our clients even borrow against their ever increasing cash values to provide more freedom of money in retirement.

Here are the attributes of the participating whole life policy with a mutually owned life insurance company:

- Ready access to money, on demand, on your terms.

- Total control over your own pool of financial value.

- No penalties or fees for early access.

- Growing death benefit.

- Income tax-free windfall to named beneficiaries.

- Cash values are contractually rising on a daily basis to match the total death benefit by age 100 of the life insured.

- Dividends, once declared are contractually guaranteed to be paid, cannot be repossessed and cannot lose value.

- These annual dividends, when chunked back into the policy to buy paid-up additions of death benefit at no additional cost, do not trigger a taxable event.

- The money that you access for asset purchases, investments, or lifestyle is not your money. Your money never leaves your control as it grows daily inside of your system.

Contrast this with how most people go about their financial lives and you'll not only see the problem, but you'll also see the process of Becoming Your Own Banker® is the solution to the problem.

When you begin to grow and maintain a pool of financial value that you own and control through a system of policies, you begin to experience a peaceful stress-free way of life financially. Your money remains safe and earns uninterrupted interest, even though you can borrow against it on demand and on your terms.

Nelson Nash often said, "You don't have to play their game anymore. You *can*, and *should* control the banking function as it relates to your needs."

Taxes and Disconnection

By virtue of you taking steps to get the bankers out of your life, you are no longer using *their* infrastructure to flow and store your money. That means minimal worry about transaction fees and more freedom from an ever-growing pool of capital that isn't generally hindered by tax policies.

When you remove money flow from their infrastructure, you also minimize crossing into territories where you have to worry about triggering taxes. That means no more thinking about capital gains, dividends, and interest taxes. The only ones you need to worry about are the ones that have been legally imposed on you. Of course, you have your goals and objectives and may decide to introduce money back into the banking system, for example, if you use policy loans to fund an unregistered stock investment that grew in value. At least, you will be well aware of what you are giving up and the tolls that come along with that.

Having a family banking system changes the dynamics of how you regularly interact with the government and banking system.

When you are consciously aware of changing the path of your money, you become aware of the consequences of what you are doing with your money.

By disconnecting from their system, you are flowing money into a legally binding unilateral contract that you own and control. Contractual guarantees are built in. The mutual life insurance company is required to fulfill them while your sole obligation is to pay the minimum contractual premium. This effectively shifts that money from the tentacles of the banking system into legally binding contracts, severing ties to "their game." Participating dividend-paying whole life insurance policies, when appropriately designed, are tax-exempt property.

Let's dive a little deeper into the 5 Ds of keeping taxes away from your wealth—the "pentagon of strategies" for defending and reducing taxes you owe now and into the future.

Now that your money is located in your own private warehouse built on top of "land" you co-own (the mutual insurance company), you are, metaphorically speaking, free to do as you please with the money that is accessible.

With every additional dollar that you pay in premium, your degree of financial control increases. While you may hear a reference to the word deposits, premiums are, in fact, payments. And premium payments are not a problem, rather they're a solution to a problem. Nelson Nash said The Infinite Banking Concept® is an exercise in one's imagination because it's impossible to place boundaries around something that is infinite. With a great coach, you can use your imagination and achieve what's possible instead of continuing to play "their game."

Premium payments going into your system come from after-tax income and then get moved into a tax-exempt environment—therefore, concepts of deferring and dividing income are no longer needed.

Properly designed policies have contractual guarantees where the total cash value must increase to match the death benefit by age 100. The total cash value increase is contractually guaranteed and, therefore, not income, so you won't get taxed on the build-up. In that specific case, concerns over defining income are also unnecessary because by contract, the total cash value increases are not income.

Can you see the shift in advantage to your court when you can secede from the current systems we have discussed thus far?

––––––––––––––––––

At this point in the book, you should definitely see the benefits of the process of Becoming Your Own Banker® and controlling the banking function as it relates to your needs.

But how does this help you when it comes time to keep taxes away from your wealth?

These policies are not a creature of the tax code. In fact, these policies were in existence long before the tax code was created and introduced in Canada. Therefore, the policy growth goes untouched by the government, unlike every other financial vehicle that produces a gain. In addition, the dividends you receive annually from the mutual life insurance company remain nontaxable when chunked back into the policy to purchase paid up additions (P.U.A.). Again, it deserves another mention that when appropriately implemented, the death benefit remains nontaxable to the named beneficiaries.

Understanding all of the attributes of this tool, ask yourself a logical question: "How much of my capital do I not want residing there?"

Yet, if you earn money inside of a taxable savings account, you will pay tax on that growth annually. And when you access your RRSP either before or during retirement, you will trigger a tax event, and depending on your withdrawal amounts, you may also trigger partial or complete claw backs from government benefits, as was the case with Henry's parents. Not to mention that money, once in the RRSP, cannot be accessed without penalty, similar to many other financial products. There's really no logical reason to trap your money in a vice.

Summary

"The Infinite Banking Concept® is an exercise in imagination, reason, logic, and prophecy." – **Nelson Nash**

Remember, your money must reside somewhere, and building wealth starts with the money you don't need to commit for living expenses. And if you're diligent, you can keep those expenses as low as possible to save the maximum. Herein lies your choice: take that extra cash and store it inside a tax-qualified plan, hoping that money is available when you need it the most. Or, you can store your money inside of a vehicle where it is private, contractually guaranteed to grow, shielded from taxation and readily accessible. Either way, you're choosing a business partner. One is the Canada Revenue Agency (CRA) or the other is a mutual life insurance company who is responsive only to the participating whole life policy owners. Which business partner do you want?

Chapter Five

A Case Study

"Question: Who is the biggest thief in the world? If you answered the Internal Revenue Service, you are correct!" – **Nelson Nash**

Ok, let's revisit our client Chris. As we established in the previous chapters, someone, or some organization will control your wealth, it might as well be you. Chris is an excellent example of someone who saw the benefit of controlling where his money resides, and how to keep taxes away from his wealth.

Please understand that as we get into the numbers below, they are used for educational purposes only, and have been overly simplified for ease of understanding.

Here is the fact pattern that we established with Chris when he came to work with us:

- Chris was 47 years old.
- Chris was a self-employed mechanical engineer.
- He earned (actually handles) $150,000 annually.
- He spent approximately $70,000 on living expenses.
- He saved $25,000 per year inside of an RRSP.
- His RRSP account value was reported at $250,000.

Now here were the primary issues Chris had:

- Chris paid too much in taxes and struggled to get by.
- His money was trapped in RRSP.
- Wanted to retire at 65 but wouldn't have enough.

In addition to attending one of our events, Chris took our advice and read R. Nelson Nash's book, titled *Becoming Your Own Banker*®, and promptly booked a clarity call with Henry for assistance. His initial concern was having enough money to retire; given what he told Henry, he feared he would run out of money during retirement. His fear was justified.

Chris made a decent living, but he grew increasingly concerned about his money being trapped in a vice, subjected to constant volatility and taxation. The assessment detailed his issues as follows:

- No access to money to invest in real estate as he desired. Chris had been educating himself in this area and lacked liquid accessible capital to get started.

- $7,000 goes to the Canadian Pension Plan, CPP, which gets removed from his income before he even gets paid as a sole-proprietor.

- Paying $50,000 in income taxes annually which includes the CPP contributions noted above.

- Upon review of his cashflow it was determined that Chris had been accelerating some debts including his mortgage $765 bi-weekly, which formed $20,000 of his $70,000 in annual living expenses.

- If he wanted to withdraw $250,000 from his RRSP, a 30% withholding tax (or $75,000) would be triggered, plus the lost opportunity cost.

Now let's talk about the Canadian Pension Plan (CPP) that Chris pays into. When you are gainfully employed and receive a T4 income, you can see that deduction for the CPP is extracted immediately, even before you get your pay cheque. You don't get to use any of that money during that pay period. You have to live a long life to receive an income equal to or greater than what you pay into the system cumulatively before you begin to access the benefit. And CPP is not a choice, but a government-mandated withdrawal from your pay cheque. If you have an employer, the employer pays half, and you pay the other. But if you are self-employed, you pay both. If you are a corporate business owner, and you draw a T4 income, you personally pay half, and your corporation pays the other half. So, if you own a business you should consult with your tax professional to determine what the best method is for you to receive income, whether it's T4, dividends, or a combination of both. But as the business owner you can only receive your maximum allowable CPP income—the portion paid by your business goes into a nebulous pile and is redistributed to other Canadian retirees.

Chris began paying into CPP when he was 24 years old. He wants to retire at age 65. So based on his gross contributions alone, by the time he reaches 65, he will have contributed about $280,000.

What does that mean?

At age 65, that means his *pre-tax* income will be around $10,000 and is taxable. Now the average life expectancy in Canada is 85 years of age. That means if Chris lives until 85, he will have received about $236,000 dollars. Simple subtraction indicates he will recoup less than what he paid gross into the plan. And if he dies before age 85, it's even worse.

Chris understood the issues but was committed to changing the process of how he handled his money. Namely, Chris was ready to "disconnect" and start growing his wealth outside the conventional mainstream method. He also grasped the severity of his problem and understood that his current financial team of accountants and advisors were unable to help him rectify his situation. He needed help keeping his hard-earned cash in his own hands to control the growth. He needed the guidance of a team who could show him a better way. Chris decided to implement The Infinite Banking Concept® and needed a coach.

He established a basis to work with Henry and here's what happened next. First they planned out what his scenario would look like by paying himself dividends from his new corporation. Second, they assessed the potential advantages of melting down his RRSP accounts strategically now that he could control his annual taxable income. Third, they examined the discretionary income Chris had been applying to his debt and other inefficient living expenses.

The result was a clear path for Chris to choose as follows:

Stage one: Chris generated $150,000 in self-employment money. By changing the *design* of his situation from self-employed to incorporating, he received a reduction in taxes of $25,000, leaving him paying only $18,000 in income taxes in his corporation. This is compared to the $43,000 that he used to pay personally.

Stage two: Chris can now change the *definition* of his income from salary to dividends. This positively impacted the amount forcibly taken for CPP. By choosing dividends, Chris pays $18,000 in taxes for the corporation. Moving forward, when he decides to access his money it can be through dividends which he pays another tax on personally. On $55,000 of dividend income his dividend tax would be $4,000. By reclassifying his income *definition* as dividends, he can opt out of further CPP contributions.

Therefore he saves another $3,000 compared to the $7,000 of what he previously contributed to the CPP.

So far, Chris has found $28,000 in savings from taxes alone! Which is fantastic, right?

Stage three: This is where we started the *disconnection* process. Previously, when sending $25,000 a year into his RRSP, Chris used to get a tax refund of approximately $11,000. Think about that carefully for a moment. He deposits $25K into an account and receives $11K in a refund. The risk is that if Chris delays the withdrawal of his RRSP, he could be paying a higher tax rate. And with the complete uncertainty of what future tax rates will be (the probability is higher), he could end up paying more in taxes at withdrawal than he saved on taxes by putting the money into an RRSP initially. So, there's a considerable risk that he won't receive any advantage on taxation by contributing to the RRSP.

Therefore, he changed where that $25,000 would reside. He committed this amount as part of the total premiums he would use to purchase dividend-paying participating whole life policies. He will never be taxed on the build-up of cash value, and the death benefit to his heirs will be income tax-free versus the 45%+ tax rate his heirs would have paid on his RRSP account fair market value if Chris had passed the day we made these changes.

What did Chris decide to do?

Chris has now been empowered with knowledge about his own circumstances and for the first time feels in control over his financial fate. He now controls how much he draws from his own corporation (whomever has the gold makes the rules). And so, he decided to draw no income from his corporation and divert a sustainable $50,000 per year into his system of dividend-paying, participating whole life policies. However, he said he still needed approximately $55,000 gross income to live. With the situation he's in now, he can control how he gets the money he needs to live, positioning himself into a lower tax bracket.

So, Chris assessed the $250,000 in his RRSP. The tax refund he received from the annual $25,000 contributions to his RRSP was about $11,000. This means he reduced $11,000 in tax payable in those previous tax years. Now, after Henry's coaching, Chris understands that when he withdraws $55,000 from his RRSP account each year, over a four to five-year period, the taxes he will pay will only be $9,500.

A common phrase you will hear about RRSP's is "don't worry, you will be in a lower income tax bracket and therefore you will pay less taxes in retirement." Clearly that did not work out for Henry's parents as indicated earlier in this book. Through these design changes, Chris removed the uncertainty of future income tax rates rising and brought the certainty of paying less tax on his RRSP withdrawals today.

With Chris using his RRSP funds for his personal income needs, more money can pile up in his corporation for ongoing usage under Chris's control. Once his RRSP's have been gradually and incrementally melted down, he can then begin paying himself dividends as noted in the stages above. Meanwhile, more of the revenue Chris generates is able to accumulate uninterrupted, and to his advantage.

So, how did Henry help Chris reduce his exposure and dependency on the banking and tax system?

Henry coached and empowered Chris to implement a combination of the 5Ds of defense:

- Chris re-designed his income from self-employed to corporate.
- Chis redefined his income as dividends.

These two steps alone saved him $28,000 in taxes!

Chris decided where his wealth would reside, and it wasn't with someone else's bank or the government. Rather, it is with a life insurance company, that he co-owns. Chris now commits $50,000 annually to his system of policies *(the product)* from his tax savings, previous RRSP contributions, and lifestyle adjustments. From this voluntary place of control, he can now implement *the process* of Becoming his Own Banker.

Real wealth can now accumulate inside this vehicle, which he can also utilize to fund his various living expenses, and recapture any third-party debt if he so chooses, once the build-up of total cash values is sufficient.

Chris's wealth grows exponentially, shielded from tax on the build-up, keeping the tax collector at bay. He has ready access to an ever increasing pool of financial value, to borrow against, on demand, on his terms,*without incurring any penalties* and without interrupting any of the *contractually guaranteed growth!* His money will grow daily within his policies, despite ongoing market fluctuations, tax changes, and economic issues because the life insurance company itself must increase the total cash value day in, day out so that it equals the total death benefit by age 100 of the life insured. That is a contractual guarantee. It is NOT an investment.

Historically, since 1936, the mutual life insurance company Chris became a co-owner of has never failed to satisfy their contractual obligations to participating policy owners! What other financial tool possesses the same track record? Exactly, none!

With Henry's coaching and good guidance, Chris has substantially reduced his taxes, kept more of his money growing daily under his control, and began accumulating wealth far beyond what he ever imagined he could. Amongst all of this, Chris' RRSP account value can now be strategically withdrawn given his much lower tax scenario. This net amount of money can be utilized for a wider set of goals controlled by him. And every cent Chris is accumulating inside his own pool of financial value, never leaves his control. In addition, he won't run out of money even if he lives beyond 85 years because he changed where his money resides. In addition to all of this, Chris has created a permanent tax-free estate value with a high-quality, dividend-paying whole life insurance firmly in place.

Summary

"Your need for finance, during your lifetime, exceeds your need for life insurance protection." – **Nelson Nash**

In the end, if you want results like Chris, we've got to have a conversation and that's included with this book, on the house, at no charge. Schedule a time to get connected with the right advisor on our team, all of whom are authorized Infinite Banking practitioners. This is not something you should address on your own. You'll need a good coach. The goal of this book is to provide insights into a process that when combined with the right tool that can change your life the way it has for thousands of others that we've been privileged to serve since 2008 across Canada (and now the United States). You can create indestructible wealth for you and future generations.

Everyone's circumstances and financial structure are unique. The clients that we have, and the clients we want to have, tell us what they truly value, and we deliver it. Working with an experienced team of designated professionals. At the end of this book, we will provide a link to set up your initial call, just like Chris did, and we encourage you to take that step.

To make the best use of everyone's valuable time, come to your meeting prepared with all your financial data. Much like a doctor needing to know all your symptoms before providing a prognosis, confirming a diagnosis, and outlining a treatment plan. We must know where you are now, where you want to be, and your commitment to getting there.

Commitment is everything!

And if you are truly committed to securing a financial future that will be both beneficial and stress free, take those first necessary steps today.

Chapter Six

Summary

"If you are even the least bit effective in accumulating wealth, you are going to find yourself engulfed in taxation." – R. Nelson Nash

---

Take a minute and read, then re-read the quote above. It's clear that taxes are going to remain a problem, now, and into the future, as we have outlined up to this point. Our mission from the get-go has been to reveal, within this book, the truth. While you're pouring your blood, sweat, and tears into a job to earn a decent living, the government has you and every other taxpayer on their radar. That's the truth. By societal design, they have you filing your tax return and engaging professionals, all at your cost, to file your taxes, for them. Isn't it crazy how they flipped the burden of work on you? It would seem cruel and unfair, to say the least.

As we learned from Nelson, "Everything begins with the way that you think." This means, if you see that the government is taking too much of your hard-earned money and using it on items you have no say in, and that this practice will only grow, then there may be a desire to change your approach. Why? Because if you don't, you will end up working and saving only to pay for the government's spending—you will earn your cake, but the government will eat most of it, so to speak.

The average Canadian family will pay 45.2% of its income on taxes this year

FRASER INSTITUTE

Breakdown of total tax bill*	
Income Taxes	15.0%
Payroll/Health Taxes	9.3%
Sales Taxes	6.8%
Property Taxes	4.0%
Profit Taxes	4.8%
Sin Taxes	1.8%
Fuel/Vehicle/Carbon Taxes	1.4%
Other Taxes	2.0%
Total tax bill	**45.2%**

JUNE 15 2022
TAX FREEDOM DAY

*based on a family income of $129,589

Source: Canadians Celebrate Tax Freedom Day on June 15, 2022. Palacios, Milagros, Fuss, Jake, Li, Nathaniel (2022, June 15). Fraser Institute. Copyright 2023.

Remember, taxation is a parasite-host scenario. The government is the parasite, and you are the host. When the parasite continues to draw blood, or in this case, money, eventually, the supply will run out. What happens to both parties at that point? Right, both the parasite and host perish. You may not be able to alter how the parasite feeds, but you can control whether or not you remain a host for the parasite to feed on. This is where the pentagon of defense comes in. For example, you cannot control the government's spending, but you can control where your money resides, and manage your financial actions, which mitigates the government's access to your wealth to fund its expenditures. Reducing the money available should alter their spending habits, at least in theory. And yes, this requires you to shift how you handle your finances in terms of thinking and practice.

Now, you may have a tax professional like a CPA or a financial advisor(s) with whom you work and have confidence. We are not here to interfere with that relationship, but we are accessible for a second opinion, and ready to add value to your existing team of professionals. The truth is that most CPAs and financial advisors do not possess the level of knowledge or experience with this tool and process. The typical arguments around whole-life policies suggest that they are expensive and that for the same death benefit amount, you can get a basic term policy for far less premium outlay. But if you owned a business that recovered all of its seed capital in a few short years and then produced an annual profit like clockwork in a tax-exempt environment, how many businesses like that would you want to own? In essence, this is what can be created with well structured whole life policy design tailored to your specific circumstances.

The fact is most are simply unaware of the true power of high cash value, dividend-paying whole life policies combined with the process called The Infinite Banking Concept®. We are armed with a product and process that when combined, puts you in a position of total and absolute control over building a financial future that is bigger than your past.

The product is a life insurance contract and so the death benefit must have merit in every case. There are many forms of life insurance (i.e. term, whole life, universal life), and so that is another reason why you should get connected with the right advisor on our team to have an important conversation and to gain clarity as it relates to your needs. Another reason why we have Chartered Accountants (CPA's) and Chartered Life Underwriters (CLU), both on and as an extension of our team, are for them to collaborate with any tax professional who may be advising you already. Our experience is that most CPAs we interact with are focused exclusively on the tax code (understandably so) and do not possess the necessary designation, training or product knowledge, and most important, should never advise you outside their purview on life insurance needs or product selection unless they are also life licensed or designated as a Chartered Life Underwriter (CLU). Doing so could get them in very hot water from a compliance, errors, and omissions standpoint. We are here to help you and to help them. We pride ourselves in our consultative approach with all professionals involved in your planning. This is where the authorized Infinite Banking practitioner comes in and is worth their weight in gold!

Understand that, added to the dynamic lives we navigate, the North American landscape is changing. There is far more unpredictability than ever before. Not sure about that? Well, think about it the following way:

- You can't control what the banks do in terms of rates and fees, including the central bank.
- You can't control whether financial markets go up or down.
- You can't control whether the housing market goes up or down.
- You can't control whether the government will spend your money wisely or increase taxes.
- You can't control whether the political climate will impact your investments.
- You can't control when you or a loved one will draw their last breath.
- You can't control the level of inflation that will be experienced over your lifetime.
- You can't control when an emergency arises that requires access to substantial liquidity.

In a world where you can't control a great deal, isn't it worth finding out about a process and the features of a tool that can put you in a position of total and absolute control? How would you feel if you gained even a modest level of control over the list above?

What's the Problem?

In the early chapters, we spelled out the issues with onerous taxation by the Canadian government. The government is taxing wildly on more things and deeper through increasing interest rates while spending beyond its means. This is driving up our national debt and placing a burden on the current and future generations to service and repay that growing debt. You have no control over any of it. You sit back, exhausted after a long day at work, and watch the government reach into your pockets and take more and more money from you, your family, and generations to come.

We can't stress enough that the current and past tax facts predict what's to come. And if the past tells us anything, we must be even more vigilant. For example, in 1993, the capital gains tax was 75% inclusive compared to the current rate of 50%; with the precedent set in 1993 and the current debt load, there is increased potential this tax could increase again. If so, this would severely penalize Canadians for selling assets when compared to the current rates. This becomes even more significant when you pass your wealth down through generations (more on that below). In addition, the government now requires you to report the sale of all real estate property including your principal residences. If they have already added an "empty home tax," making your investment in assets more costly and less financially rewarding, how much of a stretch is it to think your principal residence could be next?

Consider the first 100 years of personal income tax in Canada. According to a Fraser Institute report from 1917 to 2017, the Income Tax Act started at six pages and has ballooned to an overly complex 1412 pages. Meanwhile, the tax form you use to file each year with the CRA, has gone from 23 reporting lines to 328 lines as of 2015. How many more lines do you think will be added by the time you retire? What about the day you pass away?

Again, back to the adage, where there's money, someone else, namely the government, is trying to take it from you.

Source: Canada's Personal Income Tax Then and Now, (n.d), Fraser Institute. Copyright, 2023

Solution

As we stated previously, this isn't about you choosing one way or another. It's about enhancing your wealth and your control over it. If you like investing in real estate or cash-producing businesses, creating your own banking system will give you more significant funds and flexibility to continue those endeavors without doing anything drastically different. You are already storing money in a banking system, so why not keep it in a system you own, control, and receive annual profits from, that mimics the storage function of a bank instead?

Do you recall our discussion on the five Ds? The first four being:

- Deferring Income
- Defining Income
- Designing Income
- Dividing Income

Deferring income relates to which financial vehicles we place our monies to ensure they are taxed later. This assumes you will be in a lower tax bracket when you take the money out. But if you recall, that may not always be the case as there are many factors in the future that you do not control.

Whereas defining, designing, and dividing income address how we classify our earnings and take advantage of the laws that relate to each individual's earning situation. These methods we described early on require you to speak with a tax professional as the tax laws are incredibly nuanced and need expert interpretation and application. No one wants the non-tax professional to administer these ideas or methods. However, it bears repeating that the four Ds may work for you in sheltering your wealth from excessive taxation. And with your newfound understanding of the four Ds, you, along with your tax professional, can assess their applicability, given your situation.

Now, although those four other Ds possess merit and should be considered, the fifth D, as we explained, will be your greatest asset. And by applying it as we have described you also end up with a cash accumulating asset! Of course, employing the fifth D will require collaboration with an authorized Infinite Banking practitioner on our team.

The fifth D is all about *disconnection*. We are not talking about disconnecting from people but from your current mindset around funding your life, specifically from the current banking system. This is where we introduced Nelson Nash's concept of the family banking system through multiple participating whole life policies. It is not about life insurance. The policies' structure, design, and placement empower you to gain independence from the banking system. When you reduce your dependence on the third-party banking system you currently use and become your own banker, you effectively place yourself back in control of how your money flows in your life. And once implemented you also simplify your estate planning. The result of this change can ensure that more of your lifelong earning potential can cascade generations.

Creating your own family bank system through the implementation of the process of Becoming Your Own Banker® and the proper usage of the participating whole life tool mentioned, has been described as creating a peaceful and stress-free way of life financially. With this mindset you can protect and preserve your wealth far beyond other conventional vehicles. Remember the story Henry shared about his father and how the RRSP *did not* serve him or the wealth he managed to save? Let Henry's father's story be a cautionary tale, perhaps even a motivator for you to change the way you think about money, banks, and the government.

Where is Your Money Now?

Capture a list of all your current assets and where you are warehousing your money. Then, ask yourself these questions:

- Is your money contractually guaranteed to grow daily?
- Is there volatility in any of the financial products you currently have?
- Is there ready access to money without interrupting your own?
- Do you know what the tax rate and tax calculation will be when those financial products produce an income?
- How much will your beneficiaries pay in tax when they inherit your taxable accounts?
- Have you ever lost sleep or experienced stress because of these uncertainties?
- When a financial emergency arises, or a high-caliber opportunity pres-

ents itself, can you access money from your accounts *without* reducing the account's value, and *without* triggering any tax?

- If nothing changes regarding where your wealth resides, will you get the results you are looking for?

Think about your answers. After all, it is all about how we think. Then take the next step.

Book a complimentary value call with a coach on our team. It's easy! Scan the QR code below or visit keeptaxesaway.com

Our goal is to help you grow and keep more of your hard-earned money. We practice the very same process in our own lives everyday, in our own families, and in our businesses, with great success as do our clients.

Do you want more or less control over your wealth? Now, it's time for you to reap the benefits and keep more of your money where it belongs, with you!

Our Bonus

We've attached a bonus chapter that helps you see how the processes, product, and mindset we've shared with you will help you win in life and in death against the long arm of the tax collector and the banking system. Let's face it we will all die someday. And I think we can all agree that when we do, we want to leave our wealth to the people and causes that matter most. But have you ever asked yourself, could that money be a blessing or a burden?

It could be a burden for your family, depending on your situation and how you've handled your finances. Or, it could mean that your family ends up with far less than you intended because the government took most of what you left. Yes, your wishes and hopes could perish right along with you. But here's the kicker, they don't have to. Read our bonus chapter for the answer!

Summary

"Everything begins with the way that you think." – Jayson Lowe

How you think matters. This book was written to be an eye-opening experience and to share our valuable "wealth" of knowledge, while also incorporating elements of Nelson Nash's process known as Becoming Your Own Banker®, and how you can use that knowledge to grow and protect your wealth. Shielding your money from onerous taxation is not only legal, it's your duty to your family now and for future generations who come after you. And our team of professionals will help you apply them if they fit.

We've designed our team exclusively to serve your needs to build, preserve, multiply, and transfer your wealth while triggering the least amount of taxable events. Aside from architecting the system with you, we ensure you're not left alone; you're guided through this process to achieve your goals and objectives. We'll coach you for life, at no additional cost.

We couldn't be more excited to help you keep what you earn and watch it increase by implementing our coaching. We are building a community of financially empowered citizens. Yes, it may sound cliché, but we all win when we help each other, and we've proven that in our business and personal lives time and time again. With over 25 client interviews available in our "Infinite Banking Client Success" series on our podcast, and well over 900 five-star Google reviews, our community is constantly expanding.

The more of us who band together, the less power the mainstream banking system and the government have to impose their rules on us through implied consent. And remember, it's not just about building wealth or keeping taxes away from your wealth. It's both!

So, don't let procrastination keep you from a better financial future. Schedule a call and let's get acquainted with each other to see if we can add value to you. Contact us at **keeptaxesaway.com.**

We can, and will, help *you* achieve *your* financial goals and keep taxes away from your wealth.

Let's Talk!

Deemed Disposition

Bonus

"Nothing is certain except for death and taxes." – Ben Franklin

At some point in time, we will all pass away. Like taxes, there is no avoiding death. It's inevitable. And for most of us, when that time comes, we want our wealth to be passed to the next generations to use and build upon. But as many of us can attest, not only does one's passing create emotional turmoil, but now there may be some unsavory "family members" looking to dip their hands into the pool of money left by the deceased. No, I'm not talking about your annoying sibling or distant cousin. We are, however, talking about the Canadian government's tax arm, the Canadian Revenue Agency (CRA), which wants what you have.

Remember the Willie Sutton law; wherever wealth resides, someone will try and steal it. So you can bet those assets you left for little Johnny and Sarah aren't going to end up in their hands untouched. In fact, Johnny and Sarah may end up with little to nothing, depending on how you set things up and how much wealth you accumulated.

By placing your money in RRSP accounts, you've already learned that while you're alive, they may not be as good as the marketing claims. The balance on your statement is *not* what you will receive at the withdrawal time, even if you remove it all. Don't be deceived! These vehicles will give you far less money to work with at the withdrawal time than most realize. But in death, it's a whole different story.

If you recall, we equated the government as the parasite and our pool of money as the host. The CRA feeds off our wealth while we live and again when we die if anything's left.

At the time of death, your passing triggers a governmental tax rule titled "deemed disposition." According to this rule, you are deemed to have sold or "disposed of" all your capital property (your assets), at the fair market value at the moment of death.

For example, you die on June 10, and the fair market value of your investment property is $300,000 on June 10. The cost base is $200,000. A capital gain will be calculated as $100,000. The taxable portion of that capital gain is 50% or $50,000. If you are taxed at a 30% tax rate, your estate would have to pay $15,000 to the government for that asset in that tax year. But when your terminal tax return is fully prepared and ready to file, the market shifts in the wrong direction and your home is now worth $199,000. Will the government take that into account and readjust the taxes due? Nope. Your heirs will still owe $15,000 to the government. The fair market value of all your capital property at the moment of your death is what's utilized for the purposes of valuing the estate and any taxes due.

Now to add insult to injury, the government expects you to pay that amount in cash within a year. Who's to say your family can afford or have the funds to access that tax bill? Will the government care? Again, no. CRA accepts no substitutes for cash.

But, what if your beneficiary is your spouse? Well, this brings on a new dimension, thankfully. There is a tax rule called "first death." If one spouse passes, leaving a surviving spouse, there is a one-time tax deferred rollover to that spouse. As the surviving spouse, you can either opt out or use the deferral, but most choose to use the rollover provision. However, when that spouse dies and most likely leaves their wealth to their children, that's termed "second death," and it's when the deemed disposition rule is triggered, and asset values are assessed for taxes due.

Let's walk through a scenario that we've heard so many clients share over the years *prior* to working with us. In this scenario, you'll witness the impact of deemed disposition at the "second death," and the CRA comes knocking at the door. We will share a scenario based on a real family we have advised to amplify just how detrimental this can be.

Here are the basic facts:

- Harvey, the husband, works for himself earning $150k per year.
- Jane, the wife, is a teacher and earns $100k per year.
- They have two kids, ages 5 and 7.
- They own three properties, a primary residence and two investment properties.
- Harvey has been contributing $25,000 to his RRSP accounts and has an account value of $250,000.
- Jane contributed $18,000 to her TFSA account until she reached the maximum allowable amount of $81,500.
- Their children each have an RESP to which Jane contributes $7,000 in total.
- They own a primary home with a gain of $100,000 (exempt from tax because of the principal residence exemption) with a fair market value of $600,000.
- Investment properties are worth a combined market value greater than their cost base by $500,000. They have a combined fair market value of $1.1 million.

Harvey and Jane die today and receive their total job-related incomes of $250,000. What happens?

- The deemed disposition rule is triggered. The total family wealth from their assets plus income earned is $2,281,500.
- The amount taxable would be $750,000:
  - $500,000 of unrealized gain on properties
  - $250,000 RRSP

Making Harvey and Jane's taxable wealth $1,000,000.

At death, all of their capital property is deemed to have been sold at fair market value at the moment of their deaths. 50% of the investment property gains of $500,000 would be taxable. Meaning $250,000 would be included in taxable income. Add in the RRSP account value of $250,000, taxable income, and their total working income of $250,000. Ultimately, their total taxable income would be $750,000, placing them into the highest possible tax bracket.

What would their tax bill look like for their terminal tax returns? Harvey's tax bill would be approximately $250,000. Jane's tax bill would be roughly $85,000.

Together, their total tax liability to be paid for that year would be $335,000. Let's put this another way: Harvey and Jane's two children would have a tax bill of $335,000 on $750,000 of taxable income. That's about 45%.

But where will two minor children get the money from? The estates of the deceased must pay this tax bill in cash within that tax year. The rule deems those assets were disposed at the moment of death, but were they? No, of course not. The executor of the estates must either liquidate those assets or find cash elsewhere to pay the tax bill.

Does that pose a real problem? Yes. So what's the solution? In this case, the family had $250,000 in RRSP account value and $81,500 in a TFSA, for a total of $331,500. The only option is to liquidate those accounts to settle a substantial tax bill. But does it cover it? It does not. Other assets have to be evaluated for liquidity.

Each property has a mortgage held by the banks. The total mortgages for all of those properties amount to approximately $582,000. Mortgages are granted based on criteria such as income-to-debt ratios. However, in this scenario, Harvey and Jane are now deceased and therefore, their income is also deceased. The children are minors, ages five and seven. How will the lenders deal with this scenario?

They will demand the loans either be paid or reassigned. A mortgage cannot be assumed by minor children with no income. So what happens? The children (via the executor of the estates) must find another way to deal with the mortgage debt. But, before you think, "Oh, just sell the properties. It's no big deal!" Let's think this through.

Why have Harvey and Jane invested in the properties in the first place? Right, to create cash flow-producing and appreciable assets to leave behind to their children—creating a financial legacy. Think about the hard-earned money saved to purchase these assets, the time and expense in repairs and maintenance, dealing with tenants, and marketing. All for what? To sell it and lose all the potential future income and asset appreciation they worked for?

And to add insult to injury, do people always pass during a seller's market? What if the housing market mirrors the 1980s or 2008-2009? You could be forced to sell during the worst time in the real estate market. Unfortunately, we see it all the time when people in this position panic and give away the farm, so to speak.

Is the real problem here more apparent to you? In your mind, you could feel good about leaving behind large sums of money for your family, but unbeknownst to you, you could simultaneously place them in a world of hurt where taxes are concerned. And in the scenario with Harvey and Jane, their dreams of leaving a legacy for generations could be taken away because of the government and banks and their limited knowledge on how to plan for this scenario.

Now, understand this is just a simple numerical example; we don't have a crystal ball to predict the future. Now, with all that you've learned, can you honestly put a price on the power of controlling your finances? And how about when you pass away? Shouldn't your children have control over the assets you leave them? Shouldn't they be able to decide if and when they sell those assets and not be dictated by the banks or the government?

In the case of Harvey and Jane, the $335,000 in taxes and the $582,000 in mortgages are a lot of money. And if it were us, we would want to keep as many of those dollars for our kids, just as Harvey and Jane would. But how?

The preceding chapters discussed the benefits of protecting our wealth from being over-taxed. And by following the generally accepted practice of storing your wealth in an RRSP, you are placing your money in a cooperative bank and government vehicle, exposing yourself to paying too much in taxes. Your money is leaving you and never coming back. But not just once, multiple times. You get taxed on your income, then any after-tax monies you throw into an RRSP, property, or any asset will be taxed again when either removed or sold and when you pass.

Time and time again, the government has its hands in your pockets. Why? Because you give them access by using the financial products and vehicles that align with *their* system and plans!

Why Term Insurance Isn't the Answer

In our business, clients often say to us: "Yeah, I get the risk of taxes and mortgages to my heirs; that's why I have a term life insurance policy, and it's cheap." Stop. First, the name in it explains the poor quality of this fix. Term life is temporary. And you cannot solve a permanent problem with a temporary solution. When you open a term policy, you will pay premiums every month or annually, and then at a pre-set time (typically ten or twenty years), the cheap premium will end, and you will be forced to make a decision. Do you renew at the substantially increased premiums or look at the purchase of a new term policy?

Now at that point, you're older and may have more health issues, so guess what? Your choice may be taken away from you based on your health condition. You still need the benefit but now you have your back against the wall. Simply put, your premiums will go up for either the renewal or a new policy just by the virtue of increased age. Eventually, the drastically increasing cost of premiums at the renewal dates forces the vast majority of people to cancel these policies and give up the benefit they needed. And all the money you put out in premiums is gone—sucked up like dust in a vacuum.

Therefore, temporary term policies are not the solution for a permanent problem.

Suppose you are the owner of a corporation, a holding company, or any of the sort that involves a corporation, the problem your heirs face at death is even worse. A corporate business already pays up to 3 layers of taxes while alive, including a punishing 50% tax rate on earned passive income. Without proactive planning, the corporate shareholder on deemed disposition taxes at the time of death could end up paying percentages that are nearly 70% of the company's value in taxes!

What's the Answer?

Well, by now, you can guess where our answers are headed. When implementing The Infinite Banking Concept® through a series of participating whole life policies, you enable the following:

- An ever-increasing death benefit that is paid income tax free to your named beneficiaries, bypassing probate and the estate.
- Contractually guaranteed daily growth of cash value with zero (0) tax on the buildup.

- Ready access to capital, on demand, on your terms, without reducing the account value.

- No one asking you how you're going to use the money, or how you intent to repay it.

When it's your time to die, the policies are legally binding contracts between you and the insurance company; you have control of what happens after you pass away. With participating whole life insurance, you guarantee a future delivery of tax-free money to settle legal obligations like the tax on deemed dispositions, debts, and other liabilities while leaving a surplus of money to continue building generational wealth.

Isn't that good?

If, at this point, you're thinking, "Could this be true? "The answer is yes, it is absolutely true...

This is what Harvey and Jane did. They consumed our educational resources and content, met with our team, established a clear fact pattern, reviewed our recommendations, and took action. Yet, Harvey and Jane didn't just research "other people's opinions." They read our other books and engaged in our training. They watched us on YouTube, subscribed to our podcast at Wealth Without Bay Street and made the commitment to build a financial future that was substantially greater than their past. They took action and connected with our fantastic team. They were determined to be successful wealth builders and actively sought out coaching from individuals who understood this process.

Understand your CPA isn't trained to build wealth. They are focused on the tax code, keeping you from getting in trouble with the authorities, and are an important part of your overall picture. However, authorized Infinite Banking practitioners, like those at Ascendant Financial, are focused on customizing systems to create wealth for you, while being mindful of navigating the taxation landscape. The cherry on top: Our clients get tremendous value from the coaching we provide.

Just by changing where their money resides, the family has a combined starting death benefit of $1.2M, which will continue rising for as long as they live. They have instant cash value to use as collateral available for policy loans on demand, on their terms. Capital is readily accessible and no longer trapped in a vice.

Since the current banking system doesn't work for anyone but the banks and government, Harvey and Jane will need to change how they handle their money. By placing their cash in properly-designed participating whole life policies, they can fund their lives themselves without relying on the banks' credit system while protecting their funds from exorbitant taxation both currently and when they eventually pass away.

Getting connected with a team of professionals, like Ascendant Financial, is vital if you are a corporate business owner. The complexity of corporations is very high and requires significant consideration to evaluate the company structures, shareholders, and goals to create custom-crafted designs. Often there are even critical buy/sell considerations to be discussed if there are multiple shareholders.

When designed accordingly, some of the features the corporate owners can enjoy would be:

- Increasing a pool of capital that grows passively, bypassing the 50% passive income tax rates.
- A growing collection of money that gains momentum over time.
- Drastically drop the layers of taxes of the corporate deemed disposition from 70% down to a percentage in the teens (individual results may vary).
- At death, a significant amount of money can exit out of the corporation personally to shareholders, bypassing the personal income tax rules.
  - CPAs are like heroes to their clients when they help them tap into a particular account available for Canadian shareholders—the capital dividend account. This is a *very underutilized* and extremely powerful mechanism for Canadians. Henry has been plugged into the CPA professional community for years and even coaches other CPAs.

You've learned what Harvey and Jane were able to accomplish, but what about *you*? Can you do this too? Yes, of course, you can. But as we've stated, every individual has specific parameters and needs, and one book cannot accommodate the infinite combinations life can produce. In order to get clear about your needs and how you can implement this process, we've provided a direct link to our incredible team below.

Keeptaxesaway.com

If you work hard to provide and save with the hope of leaving something for future generations, and you want to direct where that money goes without excess worry or stress, then do yourself a favor, schedule a value call. We guarantee you will see the difference our team and ongoing coaching bring to the table. What are you waiting for? Get started now and put yourself in a position of total control! Be committed to your financial future.

References

(n.d.). Merriam-Webster Dictionary. Retrieved from https://www.merriam-webster.com/dictionary/system

Nash, Nelson (2003, January 1). Becoming Your Own Banker® 6th ed.: Infinite Banking Concepts.

Clinton, Kevin (1997, April). Implementation of Monetary Policy in a Regime with Zero Reserve Requirements. Retrieved from https://www.bankofcanada.ca/1997/04/working-paper-1997-8/

Clinton, Kevin (1997, April). Implementation of Monetary Policy in a Regime with Zero Reserve Requirements. Working Paper. Retrieved from https://www.bankofcanada.ca/wp-content/uploads/2010/05/wp97-8.pdf

Shin, Melissa (2022, April 7). Large RRSP balances, Bill C-208 addressed in 2022 budget. Retrieved from https://www.advisor.ca/tax/tax-news/large-rrsp-balances-bill-c-208-addressed-in-2022-budget/

Palacios, Milagros, Fuss, Jake, Li, Nathaniel (2022, June 15). Canadians Celebrate Tax Freedom Day on June 15, 2022. Retrieved from https://www.fraserinstitute.org/studies/canadians-celebrate-tax-freedom-day-on-june-15-2022

(n.d.) Tax Freedom Day Calculator. Retrieved fromhttps://www.fraserinstitute.org/tax-freedom-day-calculator (to calculate your tax freedom day)

Fuss, Jake, Evin, Ryan (2022, September). Taxes versus the Necessities of Life: The Canadian Consumer Tax Index. Retrieved from https://www.fraserinstitute.org/sites/default/files/canadian-consumer-tax-index-2022.pdf (Full report)

HENRY WONG • JAYSON LOWE • RICHARD CANFIELD

Manufactured by Amazon.ca
Bolton, ON

34036496R00048